AY | THURSDAY | FRIDAY

de

☐

le

board

• Proto-
type

• Test

• Learn

SPRINT

How to Solve Big Problems
and Test New Ideas
in Just Five Days

Jake Knapp

with John Zeratsky and Braden Kowitz

Simon & Schuster

New York   London   Toronto   Sydney   New Delhi

Simon & Schuster
1230 Avenue of the Americas
New York, NY 10020

First Simon & Schuster hardcover edition March 2016

SIMON & SCHUSTER and colophon are
registered trademarks of Simon & Schuster, Inc.

For information about special discounts for bulk purchases,
please contact Simon & Schuster Special Sales at
1-866-506-1949 or business@simonandschuster.com.

The Simon & Schuster Speakers Bureau can bring authors to your live event. For more information or to book an event contact the Simon & Schuster Speakers Bureau at 1-866-248-3049 or visit our website at www.simonspeakers.com.

Manufactured in the United States of America

10 9

Library of Congress Cataloging-in-Publication Data is available.

ISBN 978-1-5011-2174-6
ISBN 978-1-5011-2177-7 (ebook)

Jake:
To Mom, who helped me make castles out of cardboard
And to Holly, who picked me up when I caught the wrong bus

John:
To my grandpa Gib, who would have bought the first hundred books

Braden:
To my parents, who encouraged me to
explore the world and make it better

Contents

SPRINT

Preface

What I was doing at work wasn't working.

In 2003, my wife and I had our first child. When I returned to the office, I wanted my time on the job to be as meaningful as my time with family. I took a hard look at my habits—and saw that I wasn't spending my effort on the most important work.

So I started optimizing. I read productivity books. I made spreadsheets to track how efficient I felt when I exercised in the morning versus at lunchtime, or when I drank coffee versus tea. During one month, I experimented with five different kinds of to-do lists. Yes, all of this analysis was weird. But little by little, I got more focused and more organized.

Then, in 2007, I got a job at Google, and there, I found the perfect culture for a process geek. Google encourages experimentation, not only in the products, but in the methods used by individuals . . . and teams.

Improving team processes became an obsession for me (yes, weird again). My first attempts were brainstorming workshops with teams of engineers. Group brainstorming, where everyone shouts out ideas, is a lot of fun. After a few hours together, we'd have a big pile of sticky notes and everyone would be in great spirits.

But one day, in the middle of a brainstorm, an engineer interrupted the process. "How do you know brainstorming works?" he asked. I wasn't sure what to say. The truth was embarrassing: I had been surveying participants to see if they enjoyed the workshops, but I hadn't been measuring the actual results.

So I reviewed the outcome of the workshops I'd run. And I noticed a problem. The ideas that went on to launch and become successful were *not* generated in the shout-out-loud brainstorms. The best ideas came from somewhere else. But where?

Individuals were still thinking up ideas the same way they always had—while sitting at their desks, or waiting at a coffee shop, or taking a shower. Those individual-generated ideas were better. When the excitement of the workshop was over, the brainstorm ideas just couldn't compete.

Maybe there wasn't enough time in these sessions to think deeply. Maybe it was because the brainstorm ended with drawings on paper, instead of something realistic. The more I thought about it, the more flaws I saw in my approach.

I compared the brainstorms with my own day-to-day work at Google. My best work happened when I had a big challenge and not quite enough time.

One such project happened in 2009. A Gmail engineer named Peter Balsiger came up with an idea for automatically organizing email. I got excited about his idea—known as "Priority Inbox"—and recruited another engineer, Annie Chen, to work on it with us. Annie agreed, but she would only give it one month. If we couldn't prove that the idea was viable in that time, she'd switch to a different project. I was certain that one month wasn't enough time, but Annie is an outstanding engineer, so I decided to take what I could get.

We split the month into four weeklong chunks. Each week, we

came up with a new design. Annie and Peter built a prototype, and then, at the end of the week, we tested the design with a few hundred people.

By the end of the month, we had struck on a solution that people could understand—and wanted to use. Annie stayed on to lead the Priority Inbox team. And somehow, we'd done the design work in a fraction of the usual time.

A few months later, I visited Serge Lachapelle and Mikael Drugge, two Googlers who work in Stockholm. The three of us wanted to test an idea for video meeting software that could run in a web browser. I was only in town for a few days, so we worked as fast as we could. By the end of the visit, we had a working prototype. We emailed it to our coworkers and started using it for meetings. After a few months, the whole company was using it. (Later, a polished and improved version of that web-based app launched as Google Hangouts.)

In both cases, I realized I had worked far more effectively than in my normal daily routine or in any brainstorm workshop. What was different?

First, there was time to develop ideas independently, unlike the shouting and pitching in a group brainstorm. But there wasn't *too much* time. Looming deadlines forced me to focus. I couldn't afford to overthink details or get caught up in other, less important work, as I often did on regular workdays.

The other key ingredients were the people. The engineers, the product manager, and the designer were all in the room together, each solving his or her own part of the problem, each ready to answer the others' questions.

I reconsidered those team workshops. What if I added these other magic ingredients—a focus on individual work, time to prototype, and an inescapable deadline? I decided to call it a design "sprint."

I created a rough schedule for my first sprint: a day of sharing information and sketching ideas, followed by four days of prototyping.

Once again, Google teams welcomed the experiment. I led sprints for Chrome, Google Search, Gmail, and other projects.

It was exciting. The sprints worked. Ideas were tested, built, launched, and best of all, they often succeeded in the real world. The sprint process spread across Google from team to team and office to office. A designer from Google X got interested in the method, so she ran a sprint for a team in Ads. The Googlers from the Ads sprint told their colleagues, and so on. Soon I was hearing about sprints from people I'd never met.

I made some mistakes along the way. My first sprint involved forty people—a ridiculously high number that nearly derailed the sprint before it began. I adjusted the amount of time spent on developing ideas and the time spent on prototyping. I learned what was too fast, too slow, and finally, just right.

A couple of years later, I met with Bill Maris to talk about sprints. Bill is the CEO of Google Ventures, a venture capital firm created by Google to invest in promising startups. He's one of the most influential people in Silicon Valley. However, you wouldn't know it from his casual demeanor. On that particular afternoon, he was wearing a typical outfit of his: a baseball hat and a T-shirt that said something about Vermont.

Bill was interested in the idea of running sprints with the startups in GV's portfolio. Startups usually get only one good shot at a successful product before they run out of money. Sprints could give these companies a way to find out if they were on the right track before they committed to the risky business of building and launching their products. There was money to be made, and saved, from running sprints.

But to make it work, I'd have to adapt the sprint process. I had been thinking about individual productivity and team productivity for years. But I knew next to nothing about startups and their business questions. Still, Bill's enthusiasm convinced me that Google Ventures was the right place for sprints—and the right place for me. "It's our mission," he said, "to find the best entrepreneurs on the planet and help them change the world for the better." I couldn't resist.

At GV, I joined three other design partners: Braden Kowitz, John Zeratsky, and Michael Margolis. Together, we began running sprints with startups, experimenting with the process, and examining the results to find ways to improve.

The ideas in this book come from our entire team. Braden Kowitz added story-centered design to the sprint process, an unconventional approach that focuses on the whole customer experience instead of individual components or technologies. John Zeratsky helped us start at the end, so that each sprint would answer the business's most important questions. Braden and John had the startup and business experience I lacked, and they reshaped the process to create better focus and smarter decisions in every sprint.

Michael Margolis encouraged us to finish each sprint with a real-world test. He took customer research, which can take weeks to plan and execute, and figured out a way to get clear results in just one day. It was a revelation. We didn't have to guess whether our solutions were good. At the end of each sprint, we got answers.

And then there's Daniel Burka, an entrepreneur who founded two startups of his own before selling one to Google and joining GV. When I first described the sprint process to him, he was skeptical. As he put it later, "It sounded like a bunch of management mumbo jumbo." But he agreed to try one. "In that first sprint, we cut through the BS and made something ambitious in just a week. I was hooked." Once we won him over, Daniel's firsthand experience as a founder, and his zero tolerance for baloney, helped us perfect the process.

Since the first sprint at GV in 2012, we've adjusted and experimented. At first we thought rapid prototyping and research would only work for mass-market products. Could we move as quickly when the customers were experts in fields such as medicine or finance?

To our surprise, the five-day process held up. It worked for all kinds of customers, from investors to farmers, from oncologists to small-business owners. It worked for websites, iPhone apps, paper medical reports, and high-tech hardware. And it wasn't just for developing products. We've used sprints for prioritization, for marketing strategy, even for naming companies. Time and time again, the process brings teams together and brings ideas to life.

Over the past few years, our team has had an unparalleled opportunity to experiment and validate our ideas about work process. We've run more than one hundred sprints with the startups in the GV portfolio. We've worked alongside, and learned from, brilliant entrepreneurs like Anne Wojcicki (founder of 23andMe), Ev Williams (founder of Twitter, Blogger, and Medium), and Chad Hurley and Steve Chen (founders of YouTube).

In the beginning, I wanted to make my workdays efficient and meaningful. I wanted to focus on what was truly important and make my time count—for me, for my team, and for our customers. Now, more than a decade later, the sprint process has consistently helped me reach that goal. And I'm superexcited to share it with you in this book.

With luck, you chose your work because of a bold vision. You want to deliver that vision to the world, whether it's a message or a service or an experience, software or hardware or even—as in the case of this book—a story or an idea. But bringing a vision to life is difficult. It's all too easy to get stuck in churn: endless email, deadlines that slip, meetings that burn up your day, and long-term projects based on questionable assumptions.

It doesn't have to be that way. Sprints offer a path to solve big problems, test new ideas, get more done, and do it faster. They also allow you to have more fun along the way. In other words, you've absolutely got to try one for yourself. Let's get to work.

—Jake Knapp
San Francisco, February 2016

Introduction

One overcast morning in May 2014, John Zeratsky walked into a drab beige building in Sunnyvale, California. John was there to talk with Savioke Labs, one of Google Ventures' newest investments. He wound his way through a labyrinth of corridors and up a short flight of stairs, found the plain wooden door marked 2B, and went inside.

Now, tech companies tend to be a little disappointing to those expecting glowing red computer eyes, *Star Trek*–style holodecks, or top secret blueprints. Most of Silicon Valley is essentially a bunch of desks, computers, and coffee cups. But behind door 2B there were piles of circuit boards, plywood cutouts, and plastic armatures fresh off the 3D printer. Soldering irons, drills, and blueprints. Yes, actual top secret blueprints. "This place," thought John, "looks like a startup *should* look."

Then he saw the machine. It was a three-and-a-half-foot-tall cylinder, roughly the size and shape of a kitchen trash can. Its glossy white body had a flared base and an elegant taper. There was a small computer display affixed to the top, almost like a face. And the machine could move. It glided across the floor under its own power.

"This is the Relay robot," said Steve Cousins, Savioke's founder and

CEO. Steve wore jeans and a dark T-shirt, and had the enthusiastic air of a middle-school science teacher. He watched the little machine with pride. "Built right here, from off-the-shelf parts."

The Relay robot, Steve explained, had been engineered for hotel delivery service. It could navigate autonomously, ride the elevator by itself, and carry items such as toothbrushes, towels, and snacks to guest rooms. As they watched, the little robot carefully drove around a desk chair, then stopped near an electrical outlet.

Savioke (pronounced "Savvy Oak") had a team of world-class engineers and designers, most of them former employees of Willow Garage, a renowned private robotics research lab in Silicon Valley. They shared a vision for bringing robot helpers into humans' everyday lives—in restaurants, hospitals, elder care facilities, and so on.

Steve had decided to start with hotels because they were a relatively simple and unchanging environment with a persistent problem: "rush hour" peaks in the morning and evening when check-ins, check-outs, and room delivery requests flooded the front desk. It was the perfect opportunity for a robot to help. The next month, this robot—the first fully operational Relay—would go into service at a nearby hotel, making real deliveries to real guests. If a guest forgot a toothbrush or a razor, the robot would be there to help.

But there was one problem. Steve and his team worried that guests might not like a delivery robot. Would it unnerve or even frighten them? The robot was a technological wonder, but Savioke wasn't sure how the machine should behave around people.

There was too much of a risk, Steve explained, that it could feel creepy to have a machine delivering towels. Savioke's head designer, Adrian Canoso, had a range of ideas for making the Relay appear friendly, but the team had to make a lot of decisions before the robot would be ready for the public. How should the robot communicate with guests? How much personality was too much? "And then there's the elevator," Steve said.

John nodded. "Personally, I find elevators awkward with other humans."

"Exactly." Steve gave the Relay a pat. "What happens when you throw a robot in the mix?"

Savioke had only been in business for a few months. They'd focused on getting the design and engineering right. They'd negotiated the pilot with Starwood, a hotel chain with hundreds of properties. But they still had big questions to answer. Mission-critical, make-or-break type questions, and only a few weeks to figure out the answers before the hotel pilot began.

It was the perfect time for a sprint.

The sprint is GV's unique five-day process for answering crucial questions through prototyping and testing ideas with customers. It's a "greatest hits" of business strategy, innovation, behavioral science, design, and more—packaged into a step-by-step process that any team can use.

The Savioke team considered dozens of ideas for their robot, then used structured decision-making to select the strongest solutions without groupthink. They built a realistic prototype in just one day. And for the final step of the sprint, they recruited target customers and set up a makeshift research lab at a nearby hotel.

We'd love to tell you that we, the authors, were the genius heroes of this story. It'd be wonderful if we could swoop into any company and dish out brilliant ideas that would transform it into a breakout success. Unfortunately, we are not geniuses. Savioke's sprint worked because of the real experts: the people who were on the team all along. We just gave them a process to get it done.

Here's how the Savioke sprint went down. And if you're not a roboticist yourself, don't worry. We use this same exact sprint structure for software, services, marketing, and other fields.

First, the team cleared a full week on their calendars. From Monday to Friday, they canceled all meetings, set the "out of office" responders on their email, and completely focused on one question: How should their robot behave around humans?

Next, they manufactured a deadline. Savioke made arrangements with the hotel to run a live test on the Friday of their sprint week. Now the pressure was on. There were only four days to design and prototype a working solution.

On Monday, Savioke reviewed everything they knew about the problem. Steve talked about the importance of guest satisfaction, which hotels measure and track religiously. If the Relay robot boosted satisfaction numbers during the pilot program, hotels would order more robots. But if that number stayed flat, or fell, and the orders didn't come in, their fledgling business would be in a precarious position.

Together, we created a map to identify the biggest risks. Think of this map as a story: guest meets robot, robot gives guest toothbrush, guest falls for robot. Along the way were critical moments when robot and guest might interact for the first time: in the lobby, in the elevator, in the hallway, and so on. So where should we spend our effort? With only five days in the sprint, you have to focus on a specific target. Steve chose the moment of delivery. Get it right, and the guest is delighted. Get it wrong, and the front desk might spend all day answering questions from confused travelers.

One big concern came up again and again: The team worried about making the robot appear too smart. "We're all spoiled by C-3PO and WALL-E," explained Steve. "We expect robots to have feelings and plans, hopes and dreams. Our robot is just not that sophisticated. If guests talk to it, it's not going to talk back. And if we disappoint people, we're sunk."

On Tuesday, the team switched from problem to solutions. Instead of a raucous brainstorm, people sketched solutions on their own. And it wasn't just the designers. Tessa Lau, the chief robot engineer, sketched. So did Izumi Yaskawa, the head of business development, and Steve, the CEO.

By Wednesday morning, sketches and notes plastered the walls of the conference room. Some of the ideas were new, but some were old ideas that had once been discarded or never thought through. In all, we had twenty-three competing solutions.

How could we narrow them down? In most organizations, it would take weeks of meetings and endless emails to decide. But we had a single day. Friday's test was looming, and everybody could sense it. We used voting and structured discussion to decide quickly, quietly, and without argument.

The test would include a slate of Savioke designer Adrian Canoso's boldest ideas: a face for the robot and a soundtrack of beeps and chimes. It would also include one of the more intriguing but controversial ideas from the sketches: When the robot was happy, it would do a dance. "I'm still nervous about giving it too much personality," Steve said. "But this is the time to take risks."

"After all," said Tessa, "if it blows up now, we can always dial back." Then she saw the looks on our faces. "Figure of speech. Don't worry, the robot can't actually blow up."

As Thursday dawned, we had just eight hours to get the prototype ready for Friday's live test in the hotel. That shouldn't have been enough time. We used two tricks to finish our prototype on time:

1. Much of the hard work had been done already. On Wednesday, we had agreed on which ideas to test, and documented each potential solution in detail. Only the execution remained.

2. The robot didn't need to run autonomously, as it would eventually in the hotel. It just needed to appear to work in one narrow task: delivering one toothbrush to one room.

Tessa and fellow engineer Allison Tse programmed and tuned the robot's movements using a beat-up laptop and a PlayStation controller. Adrian put on a pair of massive headphones and orchestrated the sound effects. The "face" was mocked up on an iPad and mounted to the robot. By 5 p.m., the robot was ready.

For Friday's test, Savioke had lined up interviews with guests at the local Starwood hotel in Cupertino, California. At 7 a.m. that morning, we rigged a makeshift research lab inside one of the hotel's rooms by duct-taping a couple of webcams to the wall. And at 9:14 a.m., the first guest was beginning her interview.

The young woman studied the hotel room decor: light wood, neutral tones, a newish television. Nice and modern, but nothing unusual. So what *was* this interview all about?

Standing beside her was Michael Margolis, a research partner at GV. For now, Michael wanted to keep the subject of the test a surprise. He had planned out the entire interview to answer certain questions for the Savioke team. Right now, he was trying to understand the woman's travel habits, while encouraging her to react honestly when the robot appeared.

Michael adjusted his glasses and asked a series of questions about her hotel routine. Where does she place her suitcase? When does she open it? And what would she do if she'd forgotten her toothbrush?

"I don't know. Call the front desk, I suppose?"

Michael jotted notes on a clipboard. "Okay." He pointed to the desk phone. "Go ahead and call." She dialed. "No problem," the receptionist said. "I'll send up a toothbrush right away."

As soon as the woman returned the receiver to its cradle, Michael continued his questions. Did she always use the same suitcase? When was the last time she'd forgotten something on a trip?

Brrrring. The desk phone interrupted her. She picked up, and an automated message played: "Your toothbrush has arrived."

Without thinking, the woman crossed the room, turned the handle, and opened the door. Back at headquarters, the sprint team members were gathered around a set of video displays, watching her reaction.

"Oh my god," she said. "It's a *robot*!"

The glossy hatch opened slowly. Inside was the toothbrush. The robot made a series of chimes and beeps as the woman confirmed delivery on its touch screen. When she gave the experience a five-star review, the little machine danced for joy by twisting back and forth.

"This is so cool," she said. "If they start using this robot, I'll stay here every time." But it wasn't what she said. It was the smile of delight that we saw over the video stream. And it was what she didn't do—no awkward pauses and no frustration as she dealt with the robot.

Watching the live video, we were nervous throughout that first interview. By the second and third, we were laughing and even cheering. Guest after guest responded the same way. They were enthusiastic when they first saw the robot. They had no trouble receiving their toothbrushes, confirming delivery on the touch screen, and sending the robot on its way. People wanted to call the robot back to make a second delivery, just so they could see it again. They even took selfies with the robot. But no one, not one person, tried to engage the robot in any conversation.

At the end of the day, green check marks filled our whiteboard. The risky robot personality—those blinking eyes, sound effects, and, yeah, even the "happy dance"—was a complete success. Prior to the sprint, Savioke had been nervous about overpromising the robot's capability. Now they realized that giving the robot a winsome character might be the secret to boosting guest satisfaction.

Not every detail was perfect, of course. The touch screen was sluggish. The timing was off on some of the sound effects. One idea, to include games on the robot's touch screen, didn't appeal to guests at all.

Savioke's Relay robot.

These flaws meant reprioritizing some engineering work, but there was still time.

Three weeks later, the robot went into full-time service at the hotel. And the Relay was a hit. Stories about the charming robot appeared in the *New York Times* and the *Washington Post*, and Savioke racked up more than 1 billion media impressions in the first month. But, most important, guests loved it. By the end of the summer, Savioke had so many orders for new robots that they could hardly keep up with production.

Savioke gambled by giving their robot a personality. But they were only confident in that gamble because the sprint let them test risky ideas quickly.

The trouble with good ideas

Good ideas are hard to find. And even the best ideas face an uncertain path to real-world success. That's true whether you're running a startup, teaching a class, or working inside a large organization.

Execution can be difficult. What's the most important place to focus your effort, and how do you start? What will your idea look like in real life? Should you assign one smart person to figure it out or have the whole team brainstorm? And how do you know when you've got the right solution? How many meetings and discussions does it take before you can be sure? And, once it's done, will anybody care?

As partners at GV, it's our mission to help our startups answer these giant questions. We're not consultants paid by the hour. We're investors, and we succeed when our companies succeed. To help them solve problems quickly and be self-sufficient, we've optimized our sprint process to deliver the best results in the least time. Best of all, the process relies on the people, knowledge, and tools that every team already has.

Working together with our startups in a sprint, we shortcut the endless-debate cycle and compress months of time into a single week.

Instead of waiting to launch a minimal product to understand if an idea is any good, our companies get clear data from a realistic prototype.

The sprint gives our startups a superpower: They can fast-forward into the future to see their finished product and customer reactions, before making any expensive commitments. When a risky idea succeeds in a sprint, the payoff is fantastic. But it's the failures that, while painful, provide the greatest return on investment. Identifying critical flaws after just five days of work is the height of efficiency. It's learning the hard way, without the "hard way."

At GV, we've run sprints with companies like Foundation Medicine (makers of advanced cancer diagnostics), Nest (makers of smart home appliances), and Blue Bottle Coffee (makers of, well, coffee). We've used sprints to assess the viability of new businesses, to make the first version of new mobile apps, to improve products with millions of users, to define marketing strategies, and to design reports for medical tests. Sprints have been run by investment bankers looking for their next strategy, by the team at Google building the self-driving car, and by high school students working on a big math assignment.

This book is a DIY guide for running your own sprint to answer your pressing business questions. **On Monday,** you'll map out the problem and pick an important place to focus. **On Tuesday,** you'll sketch competing solutions on paper. **On Wednesday,** you'll make difficult decisions and turn your ideas into a testable hypothesis. **On Thursday,** you'll hammer out a realistic prototype. And **on Friday,** you'll test it with real live humans.

Instead of giving high-level advice, we dig into the details. We'll help you assemble the perfect sprint team from the people with whom you already work. You'll learn big stuff (like how to get the most out of your team's diverse opinions *and* one leader's vision), medium stuff (like why your team should spend three straight days with your phones and computers off), and nitty-gritty stuff (like why you should eat lunch at 1 p.m.). You won't finish with a complete, detailed, ready-to-ship

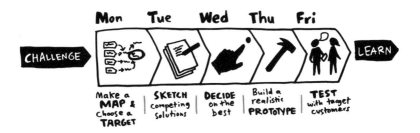

product. But you will make rapid progress, and know for sure if you're headed in the right direction.

You'll see some methods that look familiar and others that are new. If you're familiar with lean development or design thinking, you'll find the sprint is a practical way to apply those philosophies. If your team uses "agile" processes, you'll find that our definition of "sprint" is different, but complementary. And if you haven't heard of any of these methods, don't worry—you'll be fine. This is a book for experts and beginners alike, for anyone who has a big opportunity, problem, or idea and needs to get started. Every step has been tried, tweaked, tested, and measured over the course of our 100+ sprints and refined with the input we've gathered from the growing sprint community. If it doesn't work, it's not in the book.

At the end, you'll find a set of checklists, including a shopping list and day-by-day guides. You don't have to memorize everything now—the checklists await you once you're ready to run your own sprint. But before you start that sprint, you'll need to plan carefully to make it a success. In the next chapters, we'll show you how to set the stage.

Set the Stage

Before the sprint begins, you'll need to have the right challenge and the right team. You'll also need time and space to conduct your sprint. In the next three chapters, we'll show you how to get ready.

1

Challenge

In 2002, a clarinet player named James Freeman quit his job as a professional musician and founded . . . a coffee cart.

James was obsessed with freshly roasted coffee. In those days in the San Francisco area, it was nearly impossible to find coffee beans with a roast date printed on the bag. So James decided to do it himself. He carefully roasted beans in a potting shed at home, then drove to farmers' markets in Berkeley and Oakland, California, where he brewed and sold coffee by the cup. His manner was polite and accommodating, and the coffee was delicious.

Soon James and his cart, called Blue Bottle Coffee, developed a following. In 2005, he established a permanent Blue Bottle location in a friend's San Francisco garage. Over the next few years, as the business grew, he slowly opened more cafés. By 2012, Blue Bottle had locations in San Francisco, Oakland, Manhattan, and Brooklyn. It was a business that many would have considered perfect. The coffee was ranked among the best nationwide. The baristas were friendly and knowledgeable. Even the interior design of the cafés was perfect: wooden shelves, tasteful ceramic tiles, and an understated logo in the perfect shade of sky blue.

But James didn't consider the business perfect, or complete. He was still just as passionate about coffee and hospitality, and he wanted to bring the Blue Bottle experience to even more coffee lovers. He wanted to open more cafés. He wanted to deliver freshly roasted coffee to people's homes, even if they didn't live anywhere near a Blue Bottle location. If that coffee cart had been Sputnik, the next phase would be more like a moon shot.

So in October 2012, Blue Bottle Coffee raised $20 million from a group of Silicon Valley investors, including GV. James had many plans for that money, but one of the most obvious was building a better online store for selling fresh coffee beans. But Blue Bottle wasn't a tech company and James was no expert at online retail. How could he translate the magic of his cafés to smartphones and laptops?

Several weeks later, on a bright December afternoon, Braden Kowitz and John Zeratsky met up with James. They sat around a counter, drank coffee, and discussed the challenge. The online store was important to the company. It would take time and money to get it right, and it was difficult to know where to start. In other words, it sounded like a perfect candidate for a sprint. James agreed.

They talked about who should be in the sprint. An obvious choice was the programmer who would be responsible for building Blue Bottle's online store. But James also included Blue Bottle's chief operating officer, chief finance officer, and communications manager. He included the customer service lead who handled questions and complaints. He even included the company's executive chairman: Bryan Meehan, a retail expert who started a chain of organic grocery stores in the UK. And, of course, James himself would be in the room.

The online store was essentially a software project—something our team at GV was very familiar with. But this group looked almost nothing like a traditional software team. These were busy people, who would be missing a full week of important work. Would the sprint be worth their time?

On Monday morning of our sprint week, the Blue Bottle team gathered in a conference room at GV's office in San Francisco. We made a diagram on the whiteboard showing how coffee buyers might move through the online store. The Blue Bottle team targeted a new customer purchasing coffee beans. James wanted to focus the sprint on this scenario because it was so difficult. If they could establish credibility and create a great experience for someone who had never heard of Blue Bottle, let alone visited their cafés or tasted their coffee, then every other situation should be easy by comparison.

We ran into a big question: How should we organize the coffee? The shopper in this scenario would be choosing between a dozen or so varieties of bean, each in a nearly identical bag. And—unlike in Blue Bottle's cafés—there would be no barista there to help choose.

At first, the answer seemed obvious. From boutique coffee roasters to mainstream giants like Starbucks, retailers tend to organize coffee by the geographic region where it was grown. Africa, Latin America, the Pacific. Honduran coffee vs. Ethiopian coffee. It would be logical for Blue Bottle to categorize their beans the same way.

"I have to admit something," Braden announced. Everyone turned. "I'm into coffee, okay? I have a scale at home and everything." Electronic scales are the hallmark of a true coffee freak. Owning a scale meant Braden weighed the water and coffee beans so that he could experiment and adjust ratios as he brewed. We're talking science here. Coffee scales are accurate to a fraction of a gram.

Braden smiled and held his hands palm up. "I don't know what the regions mean." There was silence. We avoided looking at James. After all, Braden's brave admission might be seen as heresy.

"That's okay," said James. The floodgate opened. John and Jake didn't know the difference between coffee regions, and neither did Daniel Burka. We drank coffee together constantly, but none of us had ever admitted to our lack of sophistication.

Then Serah Giarusso, Blue Bottle's customer service lead, snapped her fingers. "What do we do in the cafés?" she asked. After all, she went on, The Braden Situation must happen to baristas all the time: a customer comes in for coffee beans, but isn't sure which kind to buy.

James is a slow and thoughtful speaker. He paused for a moment before he answered. "The brew method is very important," he said. "So we train the baristas to ask the customer a simple question: 'How do you make coffee at home?'" James explained that, depending on whether the customer used a Chemex, or a French press, or a Mr. Coffee, or whatever, the baristas could recommend a bean to match.

"'How do you make coffee at home . . . ?'" Braden repeated. Everyone jotted notes. James had started the sprint by explaining his vision: that the online store should match the hospitality of the cafés. It felt as if we were onto something.

The team spent the following day sketching ideas for the store. On Wednesday morning we had fifteen different solutions. That's too many to test with customers, so the team voted on their favorites as a way to narrow it down. Then James, the decision-maker, made the final pick of three sketches to test.

The first sketch showed a literal approach to making the website match the cafés: It looked like the inside of a Blue Bottle café, complete with wooden shelves. The second sketch included lots of text, to mirror the conversations baristas often have with customers. Finally, James chose a third sketch that organized coffee by brew method, bringing the

"How do you make coffee at home?" question right onto the computer screen.

James had chosen three competing ideas. So which one should we prototype and test? The idea of a website that looked like the café was the most appealing. Blue Bottle's aesthetic is celebrated, and a matching website would look different from anything else in the market. We had to try that idea, and it wasn't compatible with the other solutions. But those other solutions were *also* really intriguing. We couldn't quite decide.

So we decided to prototype all three. After all, we didn't need a functioning website. To appear real in our test, each fake online store only required a few key screens. Working together with the Blue Bottle team, we used Keynote presentation software to make a series of slides that looked like three real websites. With a little ingenuity, and without any computer programming at all, we stitched those screens into a prototype that our test customers could use.

On Friday, the team watched the customer interviews. One at a time, coffee drinkers shopped on several websites, with Blue Bottle's three prototypes slipped in among the competitors. (To avoid tipping off the customers, we gave each prototype a fake name.)

Patterns emerged. The store with wooden shelves, which everyone had such high hopes for? We thought the prototype was beautiful, but customers said it was "cheesy" and "not trustworthy." But the other two prototypes fared far better. The "How do you make coffee at home?" design worked seamlessly. And the "lots of text" design shocked us: People actually *read* all those words, and the extra information brought Blue Bottle's voice and expertise to life. As one customer said, "These guys know coffee."

James and the Blue Bottle team built confidence with their sprint. They were much closer to defining how their online store would work. What's more, they'd done it in a way that felt true to their principles of hospitality. They believed the online store could be an authentic Blue Bottle experience.

A few months later, Blue Bottle launched their new website, and their online sales growth doubled. The next year, they acquired a coffee subscription company. With a bigger team and new technology, they expanded the web store and began experimenting with new offerings. They knew it would take years to get the online store right—but in the sprint, they started on their path.

The bigger the challenge, the better the sprint

If you're starting a project that will take months or years—like Blue Bottle and their new online store—a sprint makes an excellent kickoff. But sprints aren't only for long-term projects. Here are three challenging situations where sprints can help:

High Stakes

Like Blue Bottle Coffee, you're facing a big problem and the solution will require a lot of time and money. It's as if you're the captain of a ship. A sprint is your chance to check the navigation charts and steer in the right direction before going full steam ahead.

Not Enough Time

You're up against a deadline, like Savioke rushing to get their robot ready for the hotel pilot. You need good solutions, fast. As the name suggests, a sprint is built for speed.

Just Plain Stuck

Some important projects are hard to start. Others lose momentum along the way. In these situations, a sprint can be a booster rocket: a fresh approach to problem solving that helps you escape gravity's clutches.

When we talk to startups about sprints, we encourage them to go after their most important problem. Running a sprint requires a lot of energy and focus. Don't go for the small win, or the nice-to-have project, because people won't bring their best efforts. They probably won't even clear their schedules in the first place.

So how big is too big? Sure, sprints work great for websites and other software challenges. But what about really large, complicated problems?

Not long ago, Jake visited his friend David Lowe, a vice president of a company called Graco that manufactures pumps and sprayers. Graco is not a small startup. They're a multinational company who have been in business for more than ninety years.

The company was developing a new kind of industrial pump—a machine used in assembly lines. David, the VP, wondered if a sprint might help lower the risk of the project. After all, it would take eighteen months and millions of dollars to design and manufacture the new pump. How could he be sure they were on the right track?

Jake doesn't know anything about industrial assembly lines, but out of curiosity, he joined a meeting with the engineering team. "I'll be honest," Jake said. "An industrial pump sounds too complicated to prototype and test in a week."

But the team wouldn't give up so easily. If limited to just five days, they could prototype a brochure for the pump's new features and try it in sales visits. That kind of test could answer questions about marketability.

But what about the pump itself? The engineers had ideas for that, too. To test ease-of-use, they could 3D print new nozzles and attach them to existing pumps. To test installation, they could bring cables and hoses to nearby manufacturing plants and get reactions from assembly line workers. These tests wouldn't be perfect. But they would answer big questions, before the pump even existed.

Jake was wrong. The industrial pump wasn't too complicated for a sprint. The team of engineers accepted the five-day constraint and used their domain expertise to think creatively. They sliced the challenge into important questions, and shortcuts started to appear.

The lesson? No problem is too large for a sprint. Yes, this statement sounds absurd, but there are two big reasons why it's true. First, the sprint forces your team to focus on the most pressing questions. Second, the sprint allows you to learn from just the surface of a finished product. Blue Bottle could use a slide show to prototype the surface of a website—before they built the software and inventory processes to make it really work. Graco could use a brochure to prototype the surface of a sales conversation—before they engineered and built the product they were selling.

Solve the surface first

The surface is important. It's where your product or service meets customers. Human beings are complex and fickle, so it's impossible to predict how they'll react to a brand-new solution. When our new ideas fail, it's usually because we were overconfident about how well customers would understand and how much they would care.

Get that surface right, and you can work backward to figure out the underlying systems or technology. Focusing on the surface allows you to move fast and answer big questions before you commit to execution, which is why any challenge, no matter how large, can benefit from a sprint.

2

Team

Ocean's Eleven, starring George Clooney and Brad Pitt,* is one of the all-time great caper movies. In the film, Danny Ocean, an ex-con played by Clooney, organizes a band of career criminals for a once-in-a-lifetime heist. Their target: a Las Vegas casino on the night of a big prizefight, when $150 million will be in the vault. The odds are against them, the clock is ticking, and it takes an intricate strategy and every special skill the team possesses to pull it off. There's a pickpocket, an explosives guy, even an acrobat. It's excellent cinema.

A sprint resembles that perfectly orchestrated heist. You and your team put your talents, time, and energy to their best use, taking on an overwhelming challenge and using your wits (and a little trickery) to overcome every obstacle that crosses your path. To pull it off, you need

---

*Or Frank Sinatra and Dean Martin, if you prefer the original.

the right team. You shouldn't need a pickpocket, but you will need a leader and a set of diverse skills.

To build the perfect sprint team, first you're going to need a Danny Ocean: someone with authority to make decisions. That person is the Decider, a role so important we went ahead and capitalized it. The Decider is the official decision-maker for the project. At many startups we work with, it's a founder or CEO. At bigger companies, it might be a VP, a product manager, or another team leader. These Deciders generally understand the problem in depth, and they often have strong opinions and criteria to help find the right solution.

Take Blue Bottle Coffee's sprint. Having CEO James Freeman in the room was critical. He was there to talk about Blue Bottle's core values and share his vision for an online store that matched their standards of hospitality. He chose the sketches that best aligned with that vision. And he knew how the baristas were trained, a detail that unlocked a surprising solution.

But it isn't just expertise and vision that makes decision-makers so crucial. There's another important reason you need them involved in your sprint, and we learned about it the hard way. See, one of the early sprints we tried was a big flop. To protect the innocent, let's call the company SquidCo.* We'll tell you who wasn't innocent: Jake, John, and Braden. We screwed up.

We'd carefully invited everyone from SquidCo's team who worked on the project. Everyone, that is, except for one person: Sam, SquidCo's chief product officer. Sam was going to be traveling, but the week worked for everybody else. So we helped SquidCo run a sprint. They

---

*We've included several stories in this book of sprints that went awry. After a lot of deliberation, we decided to use fake names for the companies and people involved. The anonymity allows us to be honest about what went wrong, without embarrassing our friends. We hope you understand.

made a prototype and tested it. The prototype did well with their customers, and the team was ready to start building.

But when Sam returned, the project ended. What happened? The solution had tested well—but Sam didn't think we had picked the right problem to solve in the first place. There were other, more important priorities for the team.

The SquidCo sprint failure was our fault. We'd tried to guess what Sam would say, and we'd failed. The Decider *should* have been in the room.

Get a Decider (or two)

The Decider must be involved in the sprint. If you, dear reader, are the Decider, clear your schedule and get in the room. If you're not, you must convince the Decider to join. You might feel nervous; after all, it's a big time commitment for a new process. If your Decider is reluctant, try one or more of these arguments:

Rapid Progress

Emphasize the amount of progress you'll make in your sprint: In just one week, you'll have a realistic prototype. Some Deciders are not excited about customer tests (at least, until they see one firsthand), but almost everyone loves fast results.

It's an Experiment

Consider your first sprint an experiment. When it's over, the Decider can help evaluate how effective it was. We've found that many people who are hesitant to change the way they work are open to a onetime experiment.

Explain the Tradeoffs

Show the Decider a list of big meetings and work items you and your team will miss during the sprint week. Tell her which items you will skip and which you will postpone, and why.

It's About Focus

Be honest about your motivations. If the quality of your work is suffering because your team's regular work schedule is too scattered, say so. Tell the Decider that instead of doing an okay job on everything, you'll do an excellent job on one thing.

If the Decider agrees to the sprint but can't spare a full week, invite her to join you at a few key points. On Monday, she can share her perspective on the problem. On Wednesday, she can help choose the right idea to test. And on Friday, she should stop by to see how customers react to the prototype.

If she's only going to make cameo appearances, your Decider needs to have an official delegate in the room. In many of our sprints with startups, the CEO appoints one or two people from the sprint team to act as Deciders when she's not there. In one sprint, the CEO sent the design director an email that read, "I hereby grant you all decision-making authority for this project." Absurd? Yes. Effective? Absolutely. This official power transfer added tremendous clarity, the kind of clarity we wish we'd had with SquidCo.

And if your Decider doesn't believe the sprint to be worthwhile? If she won't even stop by for a cameo? Hold up! That's a giant red flag. You might have the wrong project. Take your time, talk with the Decider, and figure out which big challenge would be better.*

Once you've got a Decider (or two) committed to the sprint, it's time to assemble your sprint team. These are the people who will be in the room with you, all day, every day during the sprint. On Monday, they'll work with you to understand the problem and choose which

---

*Exception to the rule: There are times when a team willfully goes *against* management because they're convinced that a prototype and real data will prove their case. If your team has decided to run a sprint without the official Decider in the room, proceed with care. We applaud your courage, but remember: Deciders are well known for squashing results when they're not in the sprint.

part to focus on. Throughout the week, they'll be the ones sketching solutions, critiquing ideas, building the prototype, and watching the customer interviews.

Ocean's Seven

We've found the ideal size for a sprint to be seven people or fewer. With eight people, or nine, or more, the sprint moves more slowly, and you'll have to work harder to keep everyone focused and productive. With seven or fewer, everything is easier. (Yes, yes—we know there were eleven people in *Ocean's Eleven*. It was just a movie!)

So who should you include? Of course you'll want some of the folks who build the product or run the service—the engineers, designers, product managers, and so on. After all, they know how your company's products and services work and they might already have ideas about the problem at hand.

But you shouldn't limit your sprint team to just those who normally work together. Sprints are most successful with a mix of people: the core people who work on execution along with a few extra experts with specialized knowledge.

In Savioke's sprint, we got great ideas from the people you'd expect, like the roboticists and the head of design. But one of the most important contributors turned out to be Izumi Yaskawa. Izumi wasn't part of the team that built the robot, but as Savioke's head of business development, she knew more than anyone about how hotels operated and what they wanted from the robot.

For Blue Bottle Coffee, important insights came from the customer service manager and the CFO, people who normally wouldn't have been involved in building the website. In other sprints, we've had winning solutions come from cardiologists, mathematicians, and farming consultants. The common traits they all shared? They had deep expertise and they were excited about the challenge. Those are people you want in your sprint.

Recruit a team of seven (or fewer)

Choosing whom to include isn't always easy, so we've created a cheat sheet. You don't have to include each and every role listed here. And for some roles, you might choose two or three. Just remember that a mix is good.

Decider

Who makes decisions for your team? Perhaps it's the CEO, or maybe it's just the "CEO" of this particular project. If she can't join for the whole time, make sure she makes a couple of appearances and delegates a Decider (or two) who can be in the room at all times.

Examples: CEO, founder, product manager, head of design

Finance expert

Who can explain where the money comes from (and where it goes)?

Examples: CEO, CFO, business development manager

Marketing expert

Who crafts your company's messages?

Examples: CMO, marketer, PR, community manager

Customer expert

Who regularly talks to your customers one-on-one?

Examples: researcher, sales, customer support

Tech/logistics expert

Who best understands what your company can build and deliver?

Examples: CTO, engineer

Design expert

Who designs the products your company makes?

Examples: designer, product manager

The word "team" is pretty cheap, but in a sprint, a team is really a *team*. You'll be working side by side for five days. By Friday, you'll be a problem-solving machine, and you'll share a deep understanding of the challenge and the possible solutions. This collaborative atmosphere makes the sprint a great time to include people who don't necessarily agree with you.

Bring the troublemaker

Before every sprint, we ask: Who might cause trouble if he or she isn't included? We don't mean people who argue just for the sake of arguing. We mean that smart person who has strong, contrary opinions, and whom you might be slightly uncomfortable with including in your sprint.

This advice is partially defensive. If the troublemaker is in the room, even just for a guest appearance, he or she will feel included and invested in the project. But there's a more important reason. Troublemakers see problems differently from everyone else. Their crazy idea about solving the problem might just be right. And even if it's wrong, the presence of a dissenting view will push everyone else to do better work.

There's a fine line between a rebel and a jerk, of course, but don't avoid people just because they disagree with you. As you'll see throughout the book, the sprint process turns competing ideas into an asset.

Often, when we list out all of the people we want in a sprint, we have more than seven. That's okay. It's a sign of a strong team! But you'll have to make tough decisions. We can't tell you which seven people to include, but we can make it easier by telling you what to do with the rest.

Schedule extra experts for Monday

If you have more than seven people you think should participate in your sprint, schedule the extras to come in as "experts" for a short visit on Monday afternoon. During their visit, they can tell the rest of the team what they know and share their opinions. (We'll tell you all about the Ask the Experts process starting on page 68.) A half an hour should be plenty of time for each expert. It's an efficient way to boost the diversity of perspectives while keeping your team small and nimble.

Now you've got your Decider, your sprinters, and some extra experts coming in for visits. Your team is all set. Except . . . oh yeah. Somebody's got to run the sprint.

Pick a Facilitator

Brad Pitt's character in *Ocean's Eleven*, Rusty Ryan, is the logistics guy. He keeps the heist running. You need someone to be the Rusty Ryan of your sprint. This person is the Facilitator, and she's responsible for managing time, conversations, and the overall process. She needs to be confident leading a meeting, including summarizing discussions and telling people it's time to stop talking and move on. It's an important job. And since you're the one reading this book, you might be a good candidate.

The Facilitator needs to remain unbiased about decisions, so it's not a good idea to combine the Decider and Facilitator roles in one person. It often works well to bring in an outsider who doesn't normally work with your team to be the Facilitator, but it's not a requirement.

This book is written to be equally handy to the Facilitator and to anyone else who's interested in sprints. If you're going to be the Facilitator, you'll find that the text speaks directly to you and the activities through which you'll lead your team, from Monday morning through Friday afternoon. But even if you're not the Facilitator, it'll all make sense to you, too.

———————

One of the great delights of watching *Ocean's Eleven* unfold is seeing how each member of the team utilizes his unique skill to help pull off the heist. You know all the characters are in the script for a reason, but you don't know exactly what they're going to do until they do it.

Sprints are the same way. Each expert in the room will provide a key contribution—whether it's background information, a fresh idea, or even a shrewd observation of your customers. Exactly what they'll say and do is impossible to predict. But with the right team in place, unexpected solutions will appear.

3

Time and Space

The typical day in the typical office goes something like this:

This day is long and busy, but it's not necessarily *productive*. Every meeting, email, and phone call fragments attention and prevents real work from getting done. Taken together, these interruptions are a wasp's nest dropped into the picnic of productivity.

There are stacks of studies about the cost of interruption. Researchers at George Mason University found that people wrote shorter, lower-quality essays when interrupted in the middle of their work. Researchers at the University of California, Irvine, reported that it takes on average twenty-three minutes for distracted workers to return to their tasks. (We plan to read more of these studies, right after we answer this text message.)

No doubt about it: Fragmentation hurts productivity. Of course, nobody *wants* to work this way. We all want to get important work done. And we know that meaningful work, especially the kind of creative effort needed to solve big problems, requires long, uninterrupted blocks of time.

That's one of the best aspects of a sprint: It gives you an excuse to work the way you want to work, with a clear calendar and one important goal to address. There are no context switches between different projects, and no random interruptions. A sprint day looks like this:

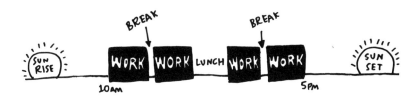

You'll start at 10 a.m. and end at 5 p.m., with an hour-long lunch in between. That's right: There are only six working hours in the typical sprint day. Longer hours don't equal better results. By getting the right people together, structuring the activities, and eliminating distraction, we've found that it's possible to make rapid progress while working a reasonable schedule.

Sprints require high energy and focus, but the team won't be able to give that effort if they're stressed out or fatigued. By starting at 10 a.m., we give everyone time to check email and feel caught up before the day begins. By ending before people get too tired, we ensure the energy level stays high throughout the week.

Block five full days on the calendar

This step is obvious, but important. The sprint team must be in the same room Monday through Thursday from 10 a.m. to 5 p.m. Friday's test starts a little earlier, at 9 a.m.

Why five days? We tried shorter sprints, but they were exhausting and didn't allow time to build and test a prototype. We've experimented with a six-week sprint, a monthlong sprint, and a ten-day sprint. We never accomplished significantly more than we did in a week. Weekends caused a loss of continuity. Distractions and procrastination crept in. And more time to work made us more attached to our ideas and, in turn, less willing to learn from our colleagues or our customers.

Five days provide enough urgency to sharpen focus and cut out useless debate, but enough breathing room to build and test a prototype without working to exhaustion. And because most companies use a five-day workweek, it's feasible to slot a five-day sprint into existing schedules.

Your team will take a short morning break (around 11:30 a.m.), an hour-long lunch (around 1 p.m.), and a short afternoon break (around 3:30 p.m.). These breaks are a sort of "pressure-release valve," allowing people to rest their brains and catch up on work happening outside the sprint.

Inside the sprint room, everybody will be 100 percent focused on the sprint's challenge. The entire team must shut their laptops and put away their phones.

The no-device rule

In a sprint, time is precious, and we can't afford distractions in the room. So we have a simple rule: **No laptops, phones, or iPads allowed.** No virtual-reality headsets. If you're reading this book in the future, no holograms. If you're reading it in the past, no Game Boys.

These devices can suck the momentum out of a sprint. If you're looking at a screen, you're not paying attention to what's going on in the room, so you won't be able to help the team. What's worse, you're unconsciously saying, "This work isn't interesting."

Going without devices can be uncomfortable at first, but it's freeing. And don't worry. You won't be completely cut off. To make sure nobody misses anything important, there are two exceptions to the no-device rule:

1. **It's okay to check your device during a break.**
2. **It's okay to leave the room to check your device.** At any time. No judgment. Take a call, check an email, tweet a Tweet, whatever—just take it outside.

We also use devices for some specific purposes: when we need to show something to the whole team, and on Thursday for prototyping. See, we're not so mean.

Let people know ahead of time that the sprint will be device-free, and also let them know that they can step out of the room at any time. That escape hatch allows busy people to participate in the sprint without losing track of their regular jobs. The combination of a clear schedule and no devices gives your team a huge supply of raw attention. To make the best use of that time and attention, you need a good workspace. It won't have to be fancy, but it will need some whiteboards.

Whiteboards make you smarter

BadgerCo (again, not the company's real name) had one of the nicest offices we'd ever seen in San Francisco. A prime location in the SoMa neighborhood, a remodeled building with exposed wood beams, polished concrete, and lots and lots of glass. But there was one problem: the whiteboard.

For starters, it was tiny. Three feet wide at the most. The surface was grayish pink from being written on and erased so many times, and that dingy haze would *not* come off, no matter what we sprayed on it. BadgerCo also suffered from a common workplace ailment: worn-out whiteboard markers. The result was gray ink on a gray background . . . not a recipe for visibility.

The whiteboard's small surface area hampered us. We drew out a map showing how customers would discover BadgerCo's new mobile app, and it filled almost all of the available space. Then BadgerCo's head of engineering started explaining how their subscription plans worked. The plan structure was important stuff, so Braden did his best to capture it on what was left of the whiteboard.

But there just wasn't room. For a few minutes, Braden tried to MacGyver his way out of it, writing cramped words in the margins and even taping notebook paper to the wall. Finally, we called time-out and walked to Office Depot to buy some of those giant poster-size Post-it notes. It cost us about an hour and a half and taught us an important lesson: Check the whiteboards before the sprint starts.

Why did we burn 90 minutes with BadgerCo just to get more writing space? We've found that magic happens when we use big whiteboards to solve problems. As humans, our short-term memory is not all that good, but our spatial memory is awesome. A sprint room, plastered with notes, diagrams, printouts, and more, takes advantage of that spatial memory. The room itself becomes a sort of shared brain for the team. As our friend Tim Brown, CEO of the design firm IDEO, writes in his book *Change by Design*: "The simultaneous visibility of these project materials helps us identify patterns and encourages creative synthesis to occur much more readily than when these resources are hidden away in file folders, notebooks, or PowerPoint decks."

Get two big whiteboards

At minimum, you'll need two big whiteboards. That will provide enough space to do most of the sprint activities (you'll still have to take photos and do some erasing and reorganizing as you go) and enough to keep the most important notes visible for the entire week. If there aren't two whiteboards already mounted to the wall in your sprint room, there are a few easy ways to add more:

Rolling Whiteboards

These come in small and giant sizes. The small ones have a lot of unusable space down by the floor, and they shake when you draw on them. The giant ones cost a lot more, but they're actually usable.

IdeaPaint

IdeaPaint is paint that turns regular walls into whiteboards. It works great on smooth walls, and less great on rough walls. One word of advice: If you use IdeaPaint, be sure to paint *all* the walls. If you don't, it's just a matter of time before somebody writes on the non-IdeaPaint wall by accident.

Paper

If you can't get hold of whiteboards, paper is better than nothing. Those poster-size Post-it notes are pricey but easy to arrange and swap when you make mistakes. Butcher paper provides serious surface area, but sticking it to the wall requires serious ingenuity.

Ideally, you should run your sprint in the same room all day, every day. Unfortunately, that's not always possible. We're surprised how many tech companies make space for foosball tables, video games, and even music rooms—all fun but seldom used—yet can't dedicate a room to their most important project. If you have to share your sprint room, try to get rolling whiteboards that you can take with you. Don't let the team's "shared brain" be erased overnight.

Even if you don't have a conference room to yourself, you can always make an ad hoc space for your sprint by using rolling whiteboards as partitions. It's kind of like you're a kid again, building a fort out of chairs and blankets. Tape stuff to walls, move around furniture—do what you have to do to create a good workspace.

Stock up on the right supplies

Before starting your sprint, you'll need a bunch of basic office supplies, including sticky notes, markers, pens, Time Timers (see below), and regular old printer paper. You'll also need healthy snacks to keep up the team's energy. We've got strong opinions about which supplies are best, so we've included a shopping list at the end of the book.

The Magic Clock

"How much longer?" In the fall of 1983, Jan Rogers was hearing this question a dozen times a day in her Cincinnati home. Her four-year-old daughter, Loran, was unusually curious about time. Jan tried every conceivable answer:

"Until the little hand moves here."

"Until the alarm dings."

"Two *Sesame Street*s."

No matter what Jan said, little Loran just didn't get it. So Jan went searching for a better clock. She tried digital clocks and analog clocks. She tried egg timers and alarms. She scoured Cincinnati's shopping malls for a clock that could make the abstract idea of time clear to a four-year-old. But none of them worked. "I'm not giving up," Jan thought. "I'll invent a clock if I have to." And that's what she did.

That evening, Jan sat down at the kitchen table with scissors and a pile of paper and cardboard and started experimenting. "That first prototype was really simple," Jan recalls. "A red paper plate cut to slide into a white paper plate. It was all manual, so I had to actually move the plates as time elapsed."

Loran got it. And Jan realized she was onto something. She called her invention the "Time Timer." At first, Jan manufactured the timers in her basement, using double-sided tape to hold the pieces together. Slowly but steadily, Jan Rogers turned the Time Timer into an enterprise. Today, Jan is CEO of a multimillion-dollar business, and you can find Time Timers in classrooms around the world, from kindergartens in Amsterdam to Stanford University.

The Time Timer itself is an object of simple beauty. True to Jan's original design, it has a red disk that moves as time elapses. It makes the abstract passage of time vivid and concrete. When Jake first saw a Time Timer, in his son's classroom, he fell in love. "Please," he said to the teacher. "Tell me where to get one of these." After all, if the timer worked for preschoolers, it should be perfect for CEOs. And it was.

We use Time Timers in our sprints to mark small chunks of time, anywhere from three minutes to one hour. These tiny deadlines give everyone an added sense of focus and urgency. Now, there are plenty of ways to keep time that don't require a special device, but the Time Timer is worth the extra cost. Because it's a large mechanical object, it's visible to everyone in the room in a way that no phone or iPad app could ever be. And unlike with a traditional clock, no math or memory is required to figure out how much time is remaining. When time is visible, it becomes easy to understand and discuss, and that's as important for a team of professionals as it was for Jan's daughter Loran.

If you're the Facilitator, using the Time Timer comes with two extra benefits. First, it makes you look like you know what you're doing. After all, you've got a crazy clock! Second, although most would never admit it, people like having a tight schedule. It builds confidence in the sprint process, and in you as a Facilitator.

Jake likes to introduce the Time Timer with a bit of narrative, because timing people while they talk can be socially awkward. He says something like:

"I'm going to use this timer to keep things moving. When it goes off, it's a reminder to us to see if we can move on to the next topic. If you're talking when the timer beeps, just keep talking, and I'll add a little more time. It's a guideline, not a fire alarm."

The first time you set it, people's eyes may get big, and blood pressure may rise a little. But give it a chance. By the afternoon, they'll be used to it, and most likely, they'll want to take it with them after the sprint.

Monday

Monday's structured discussions create a path for the sprint week. In the morning, you'll start at the end and agree to a long-term goal. Next, you'll make a map of the challenge. In the afternoon, you'll ask the experts at your company to share what they know. Finally, you'll pick a target: an ambitious but manageable piece of the problem that you can solve in one week.

4

Start at the End

Everybody knows the story of Apollo 13, but just in case, it goes like this: Astronauts head to moon, explosion on spacecraft, nail-biting return to earth. In Ron Howard's 1995 movie version, there's a scene where the team at Mission Control gathers around a blackboard to form a plan.

Gene Kranz, the flight director, wears a white vest, a flattop haircut, and a grim expression. He grabs a piece of chalk and draws a simple diagram on the blackboard. It's a map showing the damaged spacecraft's path from outer space, around the moon, and (hopefully) back to the earth's surface—a trip that will take more than two days. The goal is clear: To get the astronauts home safely, Mission Control has to keep them alive and on the right course for every minute of that journey.

Throughout the film, Kranz returns to that goal on the blackboard. In the chaos of Mission Control, the simple diagram helps keep the

Mission Control's blackboard looked sort of like this.

team focused on the right problems. First, they correct the ship's course to ensure it won't veer into deep space. Next, they replace a failing air filter so the astronauts can breathe. And only then do they turn their attention to a safe landing.

When a big problem comes along, like the challenge you selected for your sprint, it's natural to want to solve it right away. The clock is ticking, the team is amped up, and solutions start popping into everyone's mind. But if you don't first slow down, share what you know, and prioritize, you could end up wasting time and effort on the wrong part of the problem.

If Mission Control had worried about the air filter first, they would have missed their window to fix the trajectory, and the Apollo 13 spaceship might have careened off toward Pluto.* Instead, NASA got organized and sorted their priorities *before* they started on solutions. That's smart. And that's the same way your team will start your sprint. In fact

---

*Pluto, if you're reading, we still believe you're a planet.

(with the luxury of unlimited oxygen) you'll devote the entire first day of your sprint to planning.

Monday begins with an exercise we call **Start at the End**: a look ahead—to the end of the sprint week and beyond. Like Gene Kranz and his diagram of the return to planet earth, you and your team will lay out the basics: your long-term goal and the difficult questions that must be answered.

Starting at the end is like being handed the keys to a time machine. If you could jump ahead to the end of your sprint, what questions would be answered? If you went six months or a year further into the future, what would have improved about your business as a result of this project? Even when the future seems obvious, it's worth taking the time on Monday to make it specific, and write it down. You'll start with the project's long-term goal.

Set a long-term goal

To start the conversation, ask your team this question:

> "Why are we doing this project? Where do we want to be six months, a year, or even five years from now?"

The discussion could take anywhere from thirty seconds to thirty minutes. If your team doesn't quite agree about the goal or there's any lack of clarity, don't be embarrassed. But do have a discussion and figure it out. Slowing down might be frustrating for a moment, but the satisfaction and confidence of a clear goal will last all week.

Sometimes, setting the long-term goal is easy. Blue Bottle Coffee knew where they were headed in the long term: Bring great coffee to new customers online. Of course, they could have simplified their goal to "sell more coffee online," but they wanted to keep the quality of the experience high, and they wanted to challenge themselves to reach new customers, not just their existing fans. They wrote a long-term goal that reflected that ambition.

In some sprints, setting the long-term goal requires a short discussion. Savioke wanted to accomplish a lot with the Relay delivery robot. Was the goal about improving the efficiency of the front desk staff? Was it about getting as many robots in as many hotels as possible? Savioke wanted to focus on customers, and use the same goal as the hotels: better guest experience.

Your goal should reflect your team's principles and aspirations. Don't worry about overreaching. The sprint process will help you find a good place to start and make real progress toward even the biggest goal. Once you've settled on a long-term goal, write it at the top of the whiteboard. It'll stay there throughout the sprint as a beacon to keep everyone moving in the same direction.

Okay, time for an attitude adjustment. While writing your long-term goal, you were optimistic. You imagined a perfect future. Now it's time to get pessimistic. Imagine you've gone forward in time one year, and your project was a disaster. What caused it to fail? How did your goal go wrong?

Lurking beneath every goal are dangerous assumptions. The longer those assumptions remain unexamined, the greater the risk. In your sprint, you have a golden opportunity to ferret out assumptions, turn them into questions, and find some answers.

Savioke assumed their Relay robot would create a better guest experience. But they were smart enough to imagine a future where they were wrong, and the robot was awkward or confusing. They had three big questions: Can we make a smooth delivery? (the answer was yes). Will guests find the robot awkward? (the answer was no, except for the sluggish touch screen). And the long shot: Will guests come to the hotel just for the robot? (surprisingly, some people said they would).

Just like the goal, these questions guide the solutions and decisions throughout the sprint. They provide a quasi-checklist that you can refer to throughout the week and evaluate after Friday's test.

List sprint questions

You'll list out your sprint questions on a second whiteboard (if you have one). We have a few prompts for getting teams to think about assumptions and questions:

- What questions do we want to answer in this sprint?
- To meet our long-term goal, what has to be true?
- Imagine we travel into the future and our project failed. What might have caused that?

An important part of this exercise is rephrasing assumptions and obstacles into questions. Blue Bottle Coffee assumed they could find a way to convey their expertise through their website, but before the sprint, they weren't sure how. It's not difficult to find an assumption such as Blue Bottle's and turn it into a question:

Q: **To reach new customers, what has to be true?**
A: They have to trust our expertise.

Q: **How can we phrase that as a question?**
A: Will customers trust our expertise?

This rephrasing conversation might feel a little weird. Normal people don't have conversations like this one (unless they're *Jeopardy!* contestants). But turning these potential problems into questions makes them easier to track—and easier to answer with sketches, prototypes, and tests. It also creates a subtle shift from uncertainty (which is uncomfortable) to curiosity (which is exciting).

You might end up with only one or two sprint questions. That's fine. You might come up with a dozen or more. Also, just fine. If you do end up with a long list, don't worry about deciding which questions are most important. You'll do that at the end of the day on Monday, when you pick a target for the sprint.

By starting at the end with these questions, you'll face your fears. Big questions and unknowns can be discomforting, but you'll feel relieved to see them all listed in one place. You'll know where you're headed and what you're up against.

5

Map

J.R.R. Tolkien's *The Lord of the Rings* is an epic adventure, spanning three volumes and hundreds of pages. There are invented languages, histories, backstories, and subplots galore. It's an awesome story, but it's also complicated.

Frankly, it's easy to get confused while reading *The Lord of the Rings*. But Tolkien's got your back. At the beginning of the book is a map. As the characters travel through locations such as Mount Doom, the Mines of Moria, and the Misty Mountains,* the reader can flip to the map and remind herself where the action's happening and how it all fits together.

The map you'll create on Monday isn't so different: a simple diagram representing lots of complexity. Instead of elves and wizards moving

---

*For more on the Misty Mountains, refer to *Led Zeppelin IV*.

through Middle Earth, your map will show customers moving through your service or product. Not quite as thrilling, but every bit as useful.

The map is a big deal throughout the week. At the end of the day on Monday, you'll use the map to narrow your broad challenge into a specific target for the sprint. Later in the week, the map will provide structure for your solution sketches and prototype. It helps you keep track of how everything fits together, and it eases the burden on each person's short-term memory.

But there's one quality these maps do *not* have in common with the map from *The Lord of the Rings*: They're simple. No matter how complicated the business challenge, it can be mapped with a few words and a few arrows. To show you what we mean, we'd like to introduce you to Flatiron Health—a company with a very complex challenge and a very simple map.

Outside, a flurry of snow and a lead-gray cloud bank muted the Manhattan skyline, but inside, the conference room was cozy. Four of us (Jake, John, Braden, and Michael Margolis, our research partner) had traveled to New York City for a sprint with Flatiron Health, one of GV's largest investments. We were hosting the sprint at Google's office in Manhattan, a former Port Authority building that covers an entire city block. The office floor plan is confusing—Jake got lost three times on the first day—but we'd found our way to an empty room on the ninth floor, pushed the table against one wall, and gathered rolling chairs into a circle around a whiteboard.

We already knew Flatiron's backstory. The company was founded by a couple of friends, Nat Turner and Zach Weinberg. In the 2000s, Nat and Zach had built an advertising technology company called Invite Media and sold it to Google.

A few years later, the two started thinking about their next startup, and the topic of health care kept coming up. Both had seen friends and family struggling with cancer, and had witnessed, firsthand, the complexities of treatment. Nat and Zach got inspired. Large-scale data analysis, they believed, could sift through piles of medical records and test results and help doctors choose the right treatment at the right time. They left Google and started Flatiron Health.

The startup had tremendous momentum. Flatiron had raised more than $130 million in funding and acquired the industry's leading electronic medical records company. They'd hired a world-class team of engineers and oncologists and signed on hundreds of cancer clinics as customers. The pieces were in place to begin a project they believed could have a profound effect on cancer outcomes: improving clinical trial enrollment.

Clinical trials provide access to the latest treatments. For some patients, that means drugs which might save their lives. But trials aren't just about new drugs—they're also about better data. The data from every trial is collected and organized, helping researchers learn about the efficacy of new and existing therapies.

But in the United States, only 4 percent of all cancer patients are in clinical trials. The other 96 percent of cancer treatment data is unavailable to doctors and researchers who might use it to better understand the disease and better treat future patients.

Flatiron wanted to make trials available to anyone who was eligible. They hoped to build a software tool to help cancer clinics match patients to trials—a painstaking job to do manually, and perhaps the biggest hurdle to trial enrollment. Patients with common forms of cancer might qualify for trials reexamining the efficacy of standard treatment. Patients with rare forms of the disease might qualify for a new, highly targeted therapy. There were so many unique patients and so many trials that it was too much for any human to track.

The company decided to start with a sprint and had assembled a great team. The Decider was Dr. Amy Abernethy, Flatiron's chief medical officer. Nat, the CEO, was there for a few hours to give us background. Half a dozen of Flatiron's leaders joined them. There were oncologists and computer engineers, and Alex Ingram, a product manager.*

In the morning, we completed our Start at the End exercises. Choosing the goal ("More patients enrolled in clinical trials") was easy. We turned our attention to identifying the big sprint questions.

"We have to be fast," said Amy. She has an unusual accent: equal parts Australia (where she earned her PhD in medicine) and North Carolina (where she spent years running cancer research at Duke University). "If you've just been diagnosed with cancer, you can't sit around while every clinical trial is considered. You've got to start treatment *now*."

Jake uncapped his whiteboard marker and thought for a moment, trying to turn the problem into a question. Then he wrote on the whiteboard for everyone to see, *Can we find matches fast enough?*

"Each clinic already has its own ingrained process," said Alex, the product manager. "These are teams of people who have been working together in the same way for years. We've got to offer something drastically better than the status quo, or they're not going to change their workflow."

Jake added, *Will clinics change their workflow?*

With the sprint questions listed, we started on the map. Michael Margolis and Alex Ingram had interviewed staff at cancer clinics, and with help from Amy, they told us how trial enrollment worked.

To match patients with trials, doctors and research coordinators look at long lists of trial requirements: treatment history, blood count, DNA mutations in the cancer cells, and much more. As cancer care has become more sophisticated and targeted, those requirements have gotten more specific. "For a given trial, you might be talking about a handful of eligible patients across the country," said Amy. "It's like looking for needles in a haystack."

---

*If you're counting: Yes, there were more than seven people in Flatiron's sprint. It's a guideline, not an ironclad rule.

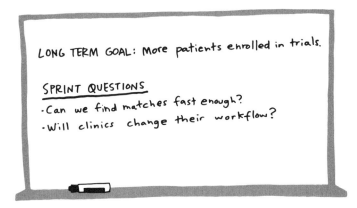

Flatiron Health's long-term goal and sprint questions.

It was an intricate and messy system. But, after an hour of discussion and a lot of revision, we were able to create a simple map:

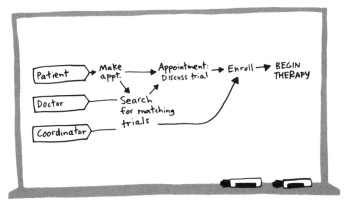

Flatiron Health's clinical trial enrollment map.

On the left was a list of the people involved in trial enrollment: the patient and the doctor (who were central to the treatment decision) and the clinic's research coordinator (who was easy to overlook but might be the best informed about trial availability). From there, the map showed the patient scheduling an appointment, the doctor and staff searching for matching trials, the appointment, the complete enrollment, and finally, the beginning of treatment.

Behind those few simple steps were all kinds of difficulties with the enrollment process: overworked staff, missing data, and communication gaps. As Amy had explained to us, many of the doctors who were supposed to suggest trials didn't even know which trials were open at their clinic. In the afternoon, we would have time to go through all of the problems and opportunities. But for now, with this map, we had enough to start.

Flatiron Health had a complicated problem and a straightforward map. Your map should be simple, too. You won't have to capture every detail and nuance. Instead, you'll just include the major steps required for customers to move from beginning to completion, in this case from cancer diagnosis to trial enrollment.

Let's look at a couple more examples. (For bonus points, see if you can spot the common elements in every map.) On Monday of their sprint, Savioke had to organize information about robotics, navigation, hotel operations, and guest habits. This is their map:

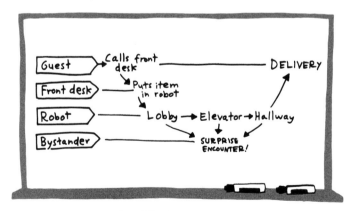

Savioke's robot delivery map.

On the first day of their sprint, Blue Bottle Coffee sorted through information about coffee selection, customer support, café operations, and distribution channels. Here is their map:

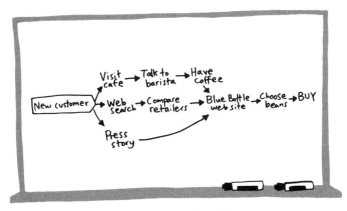

Blue Bottle Coffee's online sales map.

The common elements? Each map is customer-centric, with a list of key actors on the left. Each map is a story, with a beginning, a middle, and an end. And, no matter the business, each map is simple. The diagrams are composed of nothing more than words, arrows, and a few boxes. So now that you know what a map looks like, you're ready to make your own.

Make a map

You'll draw the first draft of your map on Monday morning, as soon as you've written down your long-term goal and sprint questions. Use the same whiteboard you wrote your goal on and dive in. When we're drawing our maps, we follow these steps (keep in mind, there's a checklist at the back of the book, so you don't have to memorize this):

1. List the actors (on the left)

The "actors" are all the important characters in your story. Most often, they're different kinds of customers. Sometimes, people other than customers—say, your sales team or a government regulator—are important actors and should be listed as well. And sometimes, of course, there's a robot.

2. Write the ending (on the right)

It's usually a lot easier to figure out the end than the middle of the story. Flatiron's story ended with treatment. Savioke's story ended with a delivery. And Blue Bottle's story ended with buying coffee.

3. Words and arrows in between

The map should be functional, not a work of art. Words and arrows and the occasional box should be enough. No drawing expertise required.

4. Keep it simple

Your map should have from five to around fifteen steps. If there are more than twenty, it's probably too complicated. By keeping the map simple, the team can agree on the structure of the problem without getting tied up in competing solutions.

5. Ask for help

As you draw, you should keep asking the team, "Does this map look right?"

You should be able to make the first quick draft of your map in thirty to sixty minutes. Don't be surprised if you continue to update and correct it throughout the day as you discuss the problem. We never get ours right the first time, but you have to start somewhere.

At this point, you will have reached an important milestone. You have a rough draft of your long-term goal, sprint questions, and map. You can already see the basic outline of your sprint: the unknowns you'll try to answer in Friday's test and the plotline of your solutions and prototype. The long-term goal is your motivation and your measuring stick.

For the rest of the day, you'll interview the experts on your team to gather more information about the problem space. As you go, you'll add more questions, make updates to your map, and perhaps even adjust the phrasing of your long-term goal. And you'll take notes as a team, to add more depth to the map on the whiteboard.

Your job on Monday afternoon will be to assemble one cohesive picture from everyone's pooled knowledge and expertise. In the next chapter, we'll give you a recipe for learning from the experts at your company, and we'll show a nearly magical way to take notes.

6

Ask the Experts

Your team knows a lot about your challenge. But that knowledge is distributed. Somebody knows the most about your customers; somebody knows the most about the technology, the marketing, the business, and so on. In the normal course of business, teams don't get the chance to join forces and use all of that knowledge. In the next set of exercises, you'll do exactly that.

Most of Monday afternoon is devoted to an exercise we call **Ask the Experts**: a series of one-at-a-time interviews with people from your sprint team, from around your company, and possibly even an outsider or two with special knowledge. As you go, each member of your team will **take notes** individually. You'll be gathering the information you need to choose the target of your sprint, while gathering fuel for the solutions you sketch on Tuesday.

Why go to all this trouble? As with many of the steps we do in sprints, we learned to do this one after making a big mistake. When we first started running sprints, we thought we could learn everything just by talking to the people in charge: usually the CEOs and managers. It makes sense. The Deciders should know the most about the project, right? Well, as it turns out, they don't know everything—even when they think they do.

We were running a sprint with WalrusCo (again, names and identifying details changed to protect the innocent). We'd already heard everything their CEO and their chief product officer had to tell us. We'd drawn our map on the whiteboard, and we were feeling confident about it. The CEO told us we "absolutely, one hundred percent" had it right.

That's when Wendy (again, name changed) stepped in the room. She was full of energy. Her shirtsleeves were rolled up to her elbows, and she rubbed her hands together and paced as she talked.

Wendy ran WalrusCo's sales team. And what she understood better than anyone was how customers reacted at different steps in the sales process. She pointed at our diagram. "Here," she said, "they're saying, 'I've never heard of this WalrusCo. Why should I trust you suckers with my account number?'" She took a swig of water from a paper cup. "Here,"—she pointed to another spot—"we're going to require their business tax ID. Nobody has that memorized. They've got to find the papers, and they're digging in their filing cabinet. If I haven't solved the trust issue by this point, game over."

Everyone jotted notes. Jake ran to the whiteboard, rubbed out a few lines with his thumb, and drew in Wendy's corrections. "Like this?" he said. Wendy looked at her watch, then checked Jake's work.

"Yeah." She crumpled her paper cup and tossed it in the trash. "About like that. Look, thanks for having me." She gave an apologetic shrug. "I got this call."

At WalrusCo, the CEO was certain we had covered everything. But Wendy changed almost every part of our map. Now, before you start thinking that WalrusCo's CEO was a goofball, we should explain that the map *was* accurate before Wendy came in. It was just more accurate afterward. Wendy put the basic facts into a real customer's context.

Nobody knows everything

What Wendy taught us was that big challenges have a lot of nuance, and to understand it all, you need to incorporate information from many sources. Nobody knows everything, not even the CEO. Instead, the information is distributed asymmetrically across the team and across the company. In the sprint, you've got to gather it and make sense of it, and asking the experts is the best and fastest way to do that.

Deciding who to talk to is a bit of an art. For your own team, you probably have a hunch about the right people already. We think it's useful to have at least one expert who can talk about each of these topics:

Strategy

Start by talking to the Decider. If the Decider is not going to be in the sprint the whole time, be sure she joins you on Monday afternoon. Some useful questions to ask: "What will make this project a success?" "What's our unique advantage or opportunity?" "What's the biggest risk?"

Voice of the Customer

Who talks to your customers more than anyone else? Who can explain the world from their perspective? Wendy is a prime example of a customer expert. Whether this person is in sales, customer support, research, or whatever, his or her insights will likely be crucial.

How Things Work

Who understands the mechanics of your product? On your sprint team, you've got the people building your product or delivering your idea—the designer, the engineer, the marketer. Savioke interviewed roboticists, Blue Bottle interviewed baristas, and Flatiron interviewed oncologists. Think about bringing in the money expert, the tech/logistics expert, and the marketing expert as well. We frequently talk with two, three, or four "how things work" experts to help us understand how everything fits together.

Previous Efforts

Often, someone on the team has already thought about the problem in detail. That person might have an idea about the solution, a failed experiment, or maybe even some work in progress. You should examine those preexisting solutions. Many sprint teams get great results by fleshing out an unfinished idea or fixing a failed one. Savioke, for instance, had nearly all the pieces of their robot personality before the sprint, but hadn't had the opportunity to assemble them.

Talking to these experts reminds the team of things they knew but may have forgotten. It always yields a few surprising insights. And the process has another nice, long-term benefit. By asking people for their input early in the process, you help them feel invested in the outcome. Later, when you begin executing your successful solutions, the experts you brought in will probably be among your biggest supporters.

Ask the Experts

Allow half an hour for each conversation, although you likely won't use all of that time. Once the expert is ready, we follow a simple script to keep things moving.

1. Introduce the sprint

If the expert isn't part of the sprint team, tell her what the sprint is about.

2. Review the whiteboards

Give the expert a two-minute tour of the long-term goal, sprint questions, and map.

3. Open the door

Ask the expert to tell you everything she knows about the challenge at hand.

4. Ask questions

The sprint team should act like a bunch of reporters digging for a story. Ask the expert to fill in areas where she has extra expertise. Ask her to retell you what she thinks you already know. And most important, ask the expert to tell you where you've got it wrong. Can she find anything on your map that's incomplete? Would she add any sprint questions to your list? What opportunities does she see? Useful phrases are "Why?" and "Tell me more about that."

5. Fix the whiteboards

Add sprint questions. Change your map. If necessary, update your long-term goal. Your experts are here to tell you what you didn't know (or forgot) in the morning, so don't be shy about making revisions.

That's it. Your experts don't have to prepare a slide deck. If they already have something to show, that's fine, but off-the-cuff discussion about the map and the customers is often more efficient. This need for improvisation is a little unnerving, but it works. If they're truly experts, they'll tell you things you wouldn't know to ask.

Your experts will provide a ton of information. So how are you going to keep track of it all? By tomorrow, when the team sketches solutions, a lot of the interesting details will have faded from your short-term memory. The whiteboards will be helpful, but they're not enough. You're going to need some additional notes.

Imagine that every person on the team took his or her own notes. That would be nice, but if one person alone had an interesting observation, the rest of the group wouldn't benefit from it. Each person's notes would be trapped in his or her notebook.

Now imagine that you are a wizard. You wave your magic wand. Sheets of paper fly out of everyone's notebooks and organize themselves into one big collection. Then the pages tear themselves into scraps. Then—remember, this is magic—the most interesting scraps separate from the rest and stick themselves onto the wall for all to see. Nice job, wizard! You organized and prioritized the group's notes, and it took no time at all.

Unfortunately, we don't know how to do any actual magic. But we do have a technique that results in organized, prioritized notes from the entire team. And it's pretty fast.

The method is called **How Might We**. It was developed at Procter & Gamble in the 1970s, but we learned about it from the design agency IDEO. It works this way: Each person writes his or her own notes, one at a time, on sticky notes. At the end of the day, you'll merge the whole group's notes, organize them, and choose a handful of the most interesting ones. These standout notes will help you make a decision about which part of the map to target, and on Tuesday, they'll give you ideas for your sketches.

With this technique, you take notes in the form of a question, beginning with the words "How might we . . . ?" For example, with Blue

Bottle, we could ask, "How might we re-create the café experience?" or "How might we ensure coffee arrives fresh?"

Some of Blue Bottle Coffee's How Might We notes.

Now, some folks* will bristle at the slightly unnatural "How might we" phrasing. After all, most people don't talk like that in real life, and, combined with writing on sticky notes, it can feel a little silly. We had the same concerns ourselves when we first learned about the How Might We method.

When we tried it, we came to appreciate how the open-ended, optimistic phrasing forced us to look for opportunities and challenges, rather than getting bogged down by problems or, almost worse, jumping to solutions too soon. And because every question shares the same format, it's possible to read, understand, and evaluate a whole wall full of these notes at once (which is what you'll do later in the afternoon).

---

*We're not naming any names, but . . . *(cough)* engineers.

Take *How Might We* notes

Every person on the team needs his or her own pad of sticky notes (plain yellow, three by five inches) and a thick black dry-erase marker.* Using thick markers on a small surface forces everyone to write succinct, easy-to-read headlines.

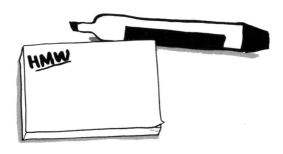

To take notes, follow these steps:

1. Put the letters "HMW" in the top left corner of your sticky note.
2. Wait.
3. When you hear something interesting, convert it into a question (quietly).
4. Write the question on your sticky note.
5. Peel off the note and set it aside.

Each person will end up with a little stack of notes—you'll organize them later.

There's no denying that this method is awkward at first, but every team we work with figures it out once they start writing. To better illustrate how all this Ask the Experts and How Might We stuff works, let's

---

*We prefer whiteboard markers over Sharpies for three reasons: (1) They're more versatile. (2) They don't smell as much. (3) If you hand Jake a Sharpie, he'll accidentally use it on the whiteboard, guaranteed.

look at part of an actual interview, and the notes that came out of it. In this scene from Flatiron's sprint, we're interviewing Dr. Bobby Green, their VP of clinical strategy. This is roughly the first two minutes of his fifteen-minute interview.

"All right, Bobby," said Jake. "What's missing on our map?"

"Well, I can talk a little more about this part." Bobby pointed to the whiteboard, where the diagram said *Search for matching trials.* "I'll give you the doctor's perspective here."

Bobby handed around a few copies of a three-page printout. "This is a typical list of criteria for a clinical trial," he said. "When we're trying to decide if a patient might be a match, we're comparing what we know about the patient to lists like this."

The pages were filled with requirements. There were fifty-four in all, everything from "Age 18 or over" to "At least four weeks since prior sargramostim (GM-CSF), interferon alfa-2b, or interleukin-2." For Jake, Braden, and John, it was tough to decipher. But the point was clear: It was a long list.

Alex Ingram, Flatiron's product manager, looked up from his printout. "The clinics don't have all of this information about their patients, right?"

Bobby nodded. "Some of these criteria are in the electronic medical record, but a lot aren't."

"Remind us how it works when the info isn't in the medical record," Amy Abernethy, Flatiron's chief medical officer, said. It was obvious that she already knew the answer, but she also knew the rest of us would benefit from hearing it.

"Well, it depends," said Bobby. "For example, many trials call for 'no uncontrolled cardiac disease.' That's pretty vague, but it probably means the patient hasn't had a recent heart attack. That kind of thing won't be easy to find in the electronic medical record. So someone from the clinic has to talk to the patient or to the patient's cardiologist. At the end of the day, the oncologist might have to make a judgment call."

Bobby set his own stack of papers on the table. "To match a patient to a trial, we've got to answer a dozen or two dozen open questions. Now multiply that by the number of new patients every week, and the number of trials at each clinic." He gave a tired smile. "And as an oncologist, you were already busy anyway."

Around the room, people nodded. Then we all wrote furiously on our sticky notes.

A recap: First, Jake, as the sprint's Facilitator, began the interview by asking Bobby about the map on the whiteboard. That gave us all context for how the new information would fit with what we'd already discussed.

Next, the team asked a lot of questions. Amy's phrase "Remind us . . ." is useful, because most interviews include content the team has heard before, at some point or another. That's okay. Covering it again refreshes everyone's memory and reveals new details. The "Remind us" phrase is also a nice way to make your expert feel comfortable. Bobby didn't need that—he's a confident public speaker—but by asking questions in this way, you can draw out great information from even the quietest person on your team.

Let's talk about note-taking. Here's a basic outline of the problems Bobby presented:

- The information required to screen patients is hard to find in their medical records.
- Filling in missing information requires a lot of time and effort.

- The number of patients, trials, and requirements is overwhelming.

Ugh. That's depressing, right? But the entire time Bobby was talking, the Flatiron team was turning those problems into How Might We opportunities. Here are some of the notes they took:

Reading the How Might We list feels a lot better than reading the problem list. It was exciting when the interviews ended and we saw each other's notes on the wall. Each How Might We note captured a problem and converted it into an opportunity.

What's more, each question could be answered in many different ways. They weren't too broad ("How might we reinvent health care?") or too narrow ("How might we put our logo in the top right corner?") Instead, Flatiron's How Might We notes were just specific enough to inspire multiple solutions. On Tuesday, they would provide the perfect inspiration for our sketches.

Bobby's interview illustrates the basic formula for Monday afternoon. You'll interview experts, using your map as an outline. You'll take notes as a team, turning each problem you hear into an opportunity. By the time you finish your interviews, your team will have generated a pile of notes. In most sprints, we end up with somewhere between thirty and a hundred. Unfortunately, you can't make good use of that many How Might We questions. Once you turn your attention to sketching, it will be too many opportunities for the poor human brain to track. You've got to narrow them down.

Organize *How Might We* notes

As soon as the expert interviews are finished, everybody should gather his or her How Might We notes and stick them on the wall. Just put them up in any haphazard fashion, like this:

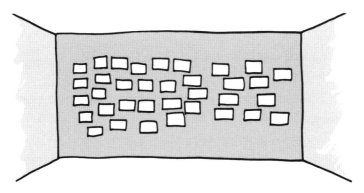

First, put up the How Might We notes without any organization.

Wow, what a mess! Now you'll organize the notes into groups. Working together, find How Might We questions with similar themes and physically group them together on the wall.

You won't know what themes to use ahead of time. Instead, the themes will emerge as you go. For example, imagine you were working with Flatiron Health. You might look at the wall and notice a few notes about electronic medical records. You'd pick those notes up and put them near each other. Bingo. You've got a theme.

As the organization goes on, it'll be useful to label the themes. Just write a title on a fresh sticky note and put it above the group. (We usually end up with a "Misc" theme of notes that don't fit anywhere else. Those misfit notes often end up being some of the best ones.)

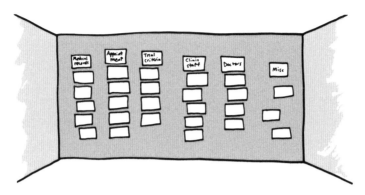

Organize into groups, and give each group a label.

This process could go on forever if you let it, but the organization doesn't have to be perfect. After ten minutes, the notes will be sorted enough to move on to prioritization.

Vote on *How Might We* notes

To prioritize the notes, you'll use dot voting. It's one of our favorite shortcuts for skipping lengthy debate. Dot voting works pretty much the way it sounds:

1. Give **two large dot stickers to each person.**
2. Give **four large dot stickers to the Decider** because her opinion counts a little more.
3. Ask everyone to **review the goal and sprint questions.**
4. Ask everyone to **vote in silence for the most useful How Might We questions.**
5. It's okay to vote for your own note, or to vote twice for the same note.

At the end of the voting, you'll have clusters of dots on a few How Might We notes, and the whole wall will be prioritized.

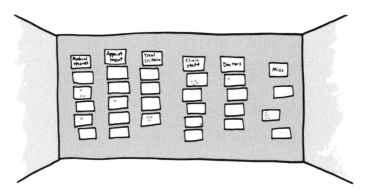

Use dots to vote for the most promising questions.

When the voting is over, take the How Might We notes with multiple votes, remove them from the wall, and find a place to stick them on your map. Most notes will probably correspond with a specific step in the story. Here's Flatiron's map again:

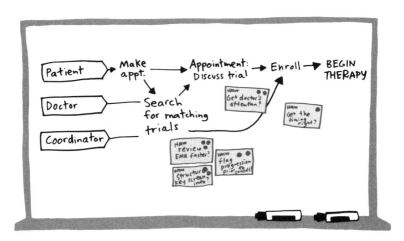

Flatiron Health's map with top How Might We notes.

The prioritization process isn't perfect: There's little time for deliberation, and early votes will sometimes bias later votes. But it leads to pretty good decisions, and it happens fast enough to leave time for the most important job of the day: After a look back over your long-term goal, your sprint questions, your map, and the notes you took this afternoon, your team will choose one specific target for the rest of your sprint's efforts.

7

Target

In 1948, a young scientist named Marie Tharp moved to New York and found a job in the geology department at Columbia University. There she took on an unusual assignment: making the world's first detailed map of the ocean floor. Tharp plotted thousands of sonar soundings with painstaking precision. Where there were gaps between data points, she used her expertise in geology and math to figure out what was missing.

As Tharp inked her map, she discovered something surprising. What had appeared to be isolated undersea mountains were in fact one long, interconnected chain of volcanic ranges and deep valleys. It jumped right out of her map: a thick, unbroken band stretching for thousands of miles.

Today, you can easily see the Mid-Ocean Ridge (as it's now known) using Google Earth. In the Atlantic Ocean the ridge shows up as a dark blue line snaking from the waters north of Greenland, through Iceland,

and all the way into the South Atlantic. There, at tiny Bouvet Island, it connects with another jagged blue band and runs east toward the Indian Ocean. On and on it goes, one ridge connecting to another, from ocean to ocean, around the entire earth.

Tharp was the first to see it. The ridge, she hypothesized, was a massive crack where the earth's shell pulled apart. At the time, plate tectonics—the idea that giant pieces of the earth's crust are in constant motion, moving continents and shaping landscapes—was generally considered to be a wacky idea. But it was difficult to argue with Tharp's map. By the late 1960s, plate tectonics was accepted as fact.

At the end of the day on Monday, you're set up for a Marie Tharp moment. Tharp didn't go looking for the Mid-Ocean Ridge, but when she compiled the data and made a map, she couldn't miss it. After interviewing the experts and organizing your notes, the most important part of your project should jump right out of your map, almost like a crack in the earth.

Your final task on Monday is to choose a target for your sprint. Who is the most important customer, and what's the critical moment of that customer's experience? The rest of the sprint will flow from this decision. Throughout the week, you'll be focused on that target—sketching solutions, making a plan, and building a prototype of that moment and the events around it.

Savioke decided to target the hotel guest (rather than the hotel staff) and to focus on the moment of delivery (rather than the elevator or lobby). The other scenarios were important, but the biggest risk and opportunity were at the guest-room door. And they knew that if they got the delivery right, they could apply what they learned elsewhere.

Blue Bottle Coffee decided to target their most challenging audience: Customers who had never heard of their cafés and who were shopping for beans they had never tasted. If they could convince strangers that their beans were worth buying, they could be sure the new online store would work well for their fans.

What about Flatiron Health? They had plenty of viable targets. They might try to help patients better understand how the clinical trials worked, and that they wouldn't be treated as guinea pigs. They might try to streamline the many steps that happened after patients agreed to a trial. They might send a message to doctors before every appointment, reminding them to consider a trial therapy. The possibilities went on and on, but Amy, the Decider, had to pick one target.

Throughout Monday afternoon, we had talked to key experts from the Flatiron team. Janet Donegan, a nurse practitioner with twenty-five years of experience in oncology clinics, gave an account of the work done by clinic staff. The software engineers—Floyd, DJ, Allison, and Charlie—detailed the world of medical record data. With each interview, the story got a little clearer.

Everyone had a chance to share an opinion about what we should focus on. Bobby Green, the VP of clinical strategy, thought it would be best to build a tool for doctors. The engineers wanted to focus on research coordinators. Both had excellent arguments.

By late afternoon, the snowfall had thickened and everyone had a cup of coffee in hand. We were all gathered around a whiteboard, where the team had drawn and redrawn (and re-redrawn) the map. The top How Might We notes were stuck beside corresponding steps in the process. To an outsider, it might have looked like a mess of arrows, text, and sticky notes. To our team, it was as clear as Gene Kranz's diagram of the Apollo 13 flight path.

At last, it was time to make the final decision about where to focus the sprint. Amy needed to choose one target customer and one target moment on the map. Those of us from GV were bracing for a long discussion. But when Jake asked Amy if she was ready, she nodded and grabbed a marker.

"Right here." Amy made two circles on the whiteboard:

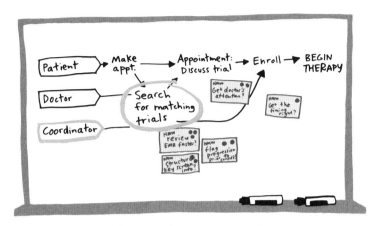

Flatiron Health's map, with target customer and target moment.

"The research coordinators," she said, "when they're searching to see if a new patient matches a trial. It's the top of the funnel, where we can evaluate the most patients. And it's the coordinators' primary job to match patients with trials. We won't be competing for attention like we would be with the doctors."

Around the room, the Flatiron team nodded, as if Amy's choice was obvious. We looked at Bobby Green. Earlier that afternoon, he'd made a great argument for focusing on doctors, since they were closer to the treatment decision. Like Amy, Bobby was an oncologist, and he'd spent years running a cancer clinic. He knew what he was talking about. But Bobby had come around. "Doctors' behavior is tough to change, and our system won't be perfect at first. The research coordinators will be more tolerant when we make mistakes."

"This is the right target," Amy said. "If we can help coordinators find more matches, it'll be a giant first step."

In all of our sprints with startups, we've never encountered anything more convoluted than clinical trial enrollment. Yet for Amy, the target was as obvious as the Mid-Ocean Ridge. It jumped right out of the map. And the rest of the team found it easy to commit to her decision.

Of course, we shouldn't have been surprised. Amy wasn't the Decider by accident. She had deep expertise and a strong vision. As for the rest of the team? Throughout the day, they had all heard the same information, seen the same notes, and agreed to the same map. Everyone had a chance to register his or her opinion. By Monday afternoon, they had clarity about the challenge, the opportunity, and the risk. The target was obvious to them, too.

Once you've clustered your team's How Might We notes, the decision about where to focus your sprint will likely be easy. It's the place on your map where you have the biggest opportunity to do something great (and also, perhaps, the greatest risk of failure).

Pick a target

The Decider needs to choose **one target customer** and **one target event** on the map. Whatever she chooses will become the focus of the rest of the sprint—the sketches, prototype, and test all flow from this decision.

Ask the Decider to make the call

It's easiest if the Decider just makes the decision without a lot of discussion and process. After all, you've been discussing and processing all day. By Monday afternoon, most Deciders will be able to make the decision as easily as Amy did. But sometimes, the Decider wants input before she chooses. If that's the case, conduct a quick, silent "straw poll" to collect opinions from the team.

Straw poll (if the Decider wants help)

Ask everyone on the team to choose the customer and the event each of them believes are most important and to write down those choices on a piece of paper. Once everyone has privately made a selection, register the votes on the map with a whiteboard marker. After the votes have been tallied, discuss any big differences of opinion. That should be enough input for the Decider. Turn it back over to her for the final decision.

Once you've selected a target, take a look back at your sprint questions. You usually can't answer all those questions in one sprint, but one or more should line up with the target. In our sprint with Flatiron, the target (coordinators searching for matching trials) matched the sprint question "Will clinics change their workflow?" By testing a solution with real coordinators, we hoped to learn the answer.

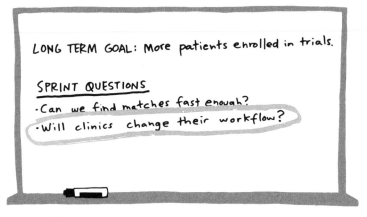

Flatiron Health's target matched one of their sprint questions.

By Monday afternoon, you've identified a long-term goal and the questions to answer along the way. You've made a map and circled the target for your sprint. Everyone on the team will have the same information, and everyone will understand the week's objective. Next, on Tuesday, it'll be time to come up with solutions.

FACILITATOR NOTES

1. Ask for permission

You may feel nervous about managing the group. That's natural. Even the most experienced Facilitators get nervous. And since structured meetings are uncommon in most companies, your team may not be used to the idea. What should you do to start things off right?

A helpful tactic (learned from our friend Charles Warren, a former Googler) is to ask the group for permission up front. Tell the team you're going to facilitate and that you'll keep track of time and process so they don't have to. Then just say, "Sound okay?"

Don't expect everyone to shout "Yes!" in unison, but because you laid it out there, and because you gave them the opportunity to object (which they likely won't), everyone will feel better about the dynamic. More importantly, so will you.

2. ABC: Always be capturing

We don't want to freak you out, but if you're playing the role of Facilitator, Monday is your busiest day. In addition to leading the group through all of the activities, you're responsible for something simple but important: recording key ideas on the whiteboard. Or as entrepreneur Josh Porter likes to say: "Always be capturing."

All day Monday, the Facilitator should have a whiteboard marker in her hand. Throughout the day, you'll synthesize the team's discussion into notes on the whiteboard. Most of the time, you'll be able to follow the exercises in this book. But not everything will fit into our templates. Feel free to improvise as you go, making lists of interesting information, drawing additional diagrams, and so on.

As you go, ask the team, "Does this look right?" or "How should I capture that?" And when the conversation starts to stall out, you can nudge it to conclusion by saying, "Is there a good way we can capture this thinking and move on?"

Remember, the whiteboard is the shared brain of the team. Keep it organized and you'll help everyone be smarter, remember more, and make better decisions, faster.

3. Ask obvious questions

The Facilitator needs to say "Why?" a lot and ask questions to which everybody already knows the answer. Covering the obvious ensures there's no misinterpretation, and it often draws out important details that not everyone knows about.

In our sprints with startups, we have an unfair advantage: We're outsiders who don't know anything, so our dumb questions are genuine. In your sprint, you'll have to act like an outsider.

4. Take care of the humans

As Facilitator, you're not only running the sprint—you've got to keep your sprint team focused and energized. Here are some of our tricks:

Take frequent breaks

Breaks are important. We like to take a ten-minute break every sixty to ninety minutes, since that's about as long as anyone can stay focused on one task or exercise. Breaks also give everyone an opportunity to have a snack and get coffee. When the team is not hungry and/or suffering from caffeine withdrawal, your job as Facilitator is much easier.

Lunch late
Eat lunch at 1 p.m., and you'll miss the rush at most cafeterias or restaurants. It also splits the day neatly in half. You'll work for three hours, from 10 a.m. to 1 p.m., then another three, from 2 p.m. to 5 p.m.

Eat light and often
Provide good, nutritious snacks in the morning and throughout the day. And be careful of eating a heavy lunch. No burritos, pizza, foot-long subs, or all-you-can-eat buffets. We learned the hard way (Indian food burritos, with tortillas made of naan) how these lunch foods can kill a group's momentum in the afternoon.

5. Decide and move on
Throughout the sprint week, there are many large and small decisions. For the biggest decisions, we've given you a script (like Monday's target, or the narrowing of sketches you'll find on Wednesday). But you'll have to handle some smaller decisions on your own.

Slow decisions sap energy and threaten the timeline of the sprint. Don't let the group dissolve into unproductive debates that aren't moving you toward a decision. When a decision is slow or not obvious, it's your job as Facilitator to call on the Decider. She should make the decision so the team can keep moving.

Tuesday

On Monday, you and your team defined the challenge and chose a target. On Tuesday, you'll come up with solutions. The day starts with inspiration: a review of existing ideas to remix and improve. Then, in the afternoon, each person will sketch, following a four-step process that emphasizes critical thinking over artistry. Later in the week, the best of these sketches will form the plan for your prototype and test. We hope you had a good night's sleep and a balanced breakfast, because Tuesday is an important day.

8

Remix and Improve

Imagine it's the early 1900s. You're drinking a nice hot cup of coffee. Only . . . it's not so nice. Coffee grounds stick in your teeth, and the liquid is so bitter your mouth puckers. If it weren't for the caffeine, you probably wouldn't bother. Back in those days, coffee was brewed like tea, by dunking a pouch of ground beans into boiling water. There was a lot of room for error: over-brewing, under-brewing, and plenty of grit at the bottom of the cup. Some people strained their coffee through filters made of cloth, but the material was overly porous and a mess to clean up.

In 1908, a German woman named Melitta Bentz got fed up with gritty, bitter coffee. Convinced there had to be a better way, Bentz went looking for ideas. She came across the blotting paper in her son's school notebook. The material was designed for mopping up excess ink. It was thick and absorbent—and disposable.

Inspired, Bentz tore out a sheet of the blotting paper. She punctured holes in a brass pot with a nail, placed the pot on top of a cup, put the paper inside, filled it with ground coffee, and added hot water. The resulting drink was smooth, grit-free, and a snap to clean up after. Bentz had invented the paper coffee filter. More than a hundred years later, it remains one of the most popular (and best) tools for brewing coffee.

We all want a flash of divine inspiration that changes the world—and impresses our teammates. We want to create something completely new. But amazing ideas don't happen like that. The lesson of Melitta Bentz is that great innovation is built on existing ideas, repurposed with vision. Coffee filters had been tried before, but they were made of cloth. And the blotting paper? It was just sitting there.

This combination of existing ideas doesn't take anything away from Bentz's achievement, but it is promising news for the rest of us would-be inventors. In your sprint, you'll follow her example: remix and improve—but never blindly copy.

You'll begin Tuesday morning by searching for existing ideas you can use in the afternoon to inform your solution. It's like playing with Lego bricks: first gather useful components, then convert them into something original and new.

Our method for collecting and synthesizing these existing ideas is an exercise we call **Lightning Demos**. Your team will take turns giving **three-minute tours** of their favorite solutions: from other products, from different domains, and from within your own company. This exercise is about finding raw materials, not about copying your competitors. We've found limited benefit in looking at products from the same industry. Time and time again, the ideas that spark the best solutions come from similar problems in different environments.

Blue Bottle wanted to help customers find coffee they'd love. But coffee beans all look alike, so photos wouldn't be helpful. To find useful solutions, the team did Lightning Demos of websites selling everything from clothes to wine, looking for ways to describe sensory details such as flavor, aroma, and texture.

In the end, it was a chocolate-bar wrapper that provided the most useful idea. Tcho is a chocolate manufacturer in Berkeley, California. Printed on the wrapper of every Tcho bar is a simple flavor wheel with just six words: Bright, Fruity, Floral, Earthy, Nutty, and Chocolatey. When Blue Bottle looked at that wheel, they got inspired, and when we sketched, someone repurposed the idea as a simple flavor vocabulary for describing Blue Bottle's coffee beans:

> The U.S.
>
> How it tastes
> Rich, chocolatey, comforting
>
> How to make it

In Friday's test, and later, at the new online store, customers loved the simple descriptions. It's a prime example of finding inspiration outside your domain (and yet another reason to be grateful for chocolate).

Sometimes, the best way to broaden your search is to look inside your own organization. Great solutions often come along at the wrong time, and the sprint can be a perfect opportunity to rejuvenate them. Also look for ideas that are in progress but unfinished—and even old ideas that have been abandoned. In Savioke's sprint, an unfinished design for the robot's eyes became the heart of the Relay's personality.

Savioke wanted to avoid the expectations of fictional robots who can carry on conversations and think independently. Both Steve, the CEO, and Adrian, the head designer, were convinced they could convey

97

the right feeling with just a pair of eyes. So on Tuesday morning of our sprint with Savioke, we spent an hour looking at eyes. We reviewed the eyes of robots in movies. We reviewed the eyes of animated characters. One stood out: a nontalking cartoon creature from the Japanese movie *My Neighbor Totoro*, who conveyed a peaceful expression with a placid, slow-moving gaze.

But the eyes that won our hearts had been there all along. Adrian showed us a variety of styles he had created long before the sprint. One design had the peaceful manner of the *Totoro* creature, combined with a simple visual style that perfectly fit the robot's aesthetic. In Friday's test, those simple blinking eyes conveyed a friendly personality, without promising conversation.

Like Savioke, you and your team should look far afield and close to home in your search for existing solutions. If you do, you're sure to uncover surprising and useful ideas.

Lightning Demos

Lightning Demos are pretty informal. Here's how they work:

Make a list

Ask everyone on your team to come up with a list of products or services to review for inspiring solutions. (Coming up with these lists on the spot is easier than it sounds—but if you like, you can assign it as homework on Monday night.) Remind people to think outside of your industry or field, and to consider inspiration from within the company. In Flatiron's sprint, the team looked at products in the medical field, such as websites for clinical trials and software that analyzed DNA. But they also looked at similar problems in different fields. They looked at tools for filtering email, task apps that sorted to-dos, management software that sorted projects and deadlines, and even the way airlines let passengers configure flight notifications. Finally, they looked at experimental projects that their own engineers had built, but not quite finished.

Everything you review should contain something good you can learn from. It's not helpful to review crummy products. After a few minutes of thinking, everyone should narrow down to his or her top one or two products. Write the collected list on the whiteboard. It's time to begin the demos.

Give three-minute demos

One at a time, the person who suggested each product gives a tour—showing the whole team what's so cool about it. It's a good idea to keep a timer going: Each tour should be around three minutes long. (In case you're wondering, yes, you can use laptops, phones, and other devices for these tours. We like to connect them to a big screen so everyone can easily see.)

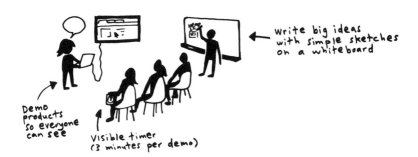

Write big ideas with simple sketches on a whiteboard

Demo products so everyone can see

Visible timer (3 minutes per demo)

Capture big ideas as you go

Your three-minute Lightning Demos will go by quickly, and you don't want to rely on short-term memory to keep track of all the good ideas. Remember the "Always be capturing" mantra and take notes on the whiteboard as you go. Start by asking the person who's giving the tour, "What's the big idea here that might be useful?" Then make a quick drawing of that inspiring component, write a simple headline above it, and note the source underneath.

For example, someone from the Flatiron team thought it would be interesting to see how comments worked in Google spreadsheets, in case we wanted to add commenting to our clinical trial matching tool. We quickly demonstrated the software, wrote the big idea ("Inline Commenting"), and jotted a quick drawing:

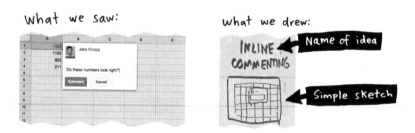

These notes are just to jog your memory later in the day, so they don't have to be fancy or detailed. We usually end up with a whiteboard full of ideas, such as this one from Flatiron's sprint:

Flatiron found plenty of interesting elements, but in the end they discarded most of them. If you record on the whiteboard as you go, you don't have to decide which ideas should be discarded and which are worth remixing and improving. You can figure that out later, when you sketch—a much more efficient use of your energy. For now, don't make decisions and don't debate. Just capture anything that *might* be useful.

By the end of your Lightning Demos, you should have a whiteboard full of ten to twenty ideas. That's enough to make sure you've captured each person's best inspiration—but it's a small enough set that you won't be overwhelmed when you start to sketch. Like the ideas on Flatiron's list, most won't turn into anything, but one or two may inspire a great solution. If you look hard enough, you can usually find your blotting paper.

When you combine the ideas you just captured with Monday's map, your sprint questions, and your How Might We notes, you've got a wealth of raw material. In the afternoon, you'll turn that raw material into solutions. But before you do, you need to form a quick strategy. Should your team split up to tackle different parts of the problem, or should you all focus on the same spot?

Blue Bottle Coffee had one specific target for their sprint: helping customers choose beans. But there were several smaller pieces of the website that were involved: the home page, the list of coffees, and the shopping cart. Without a plan, every person in the sprint might sketch the same part—say, the home page—leaving Blue Bottle without enough ideas for a whole prototype. So they divided up. Each person picked a spot, then the team checked the distribution on the map (page 102).

As you can see, the distribution wasn't even, but the team was spread out enough to ensure there would be at least a couple of solutions for each important part.

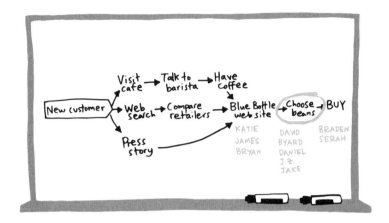

Divide or swarm

Should you divide the problem? Take a good look at your map and have a quick team discussion. If you've picked a super-focused target, it might be fine to skip assignments and have the whole team swarm the same part of your problem. If there are several key pieces to cover, you should divide up.

If you do decide to divide up, the easiest approach is to ask each person to write down the part he or she is most interested in. Then go around the room and mark each person's name next to the piece of the map that person wants to tackle in the sketches. If you end up with too many people on one spot and not enough on another, ask for volunteers to switch.

Once each person knows his or her assignment, it's time to get yourself some lunch. You'll need energy for the afternoon, because after all of your preparation, you're finally going to get a chance to sketch some solutions.

Wait a minute. Did somebody say "sketch"?

9

Sketch

Serah Giarusso, Blue Bottle Coffee's customer support lead, looked uneasy. And she wasn't the only one. James Freeman, the CEO, furrowed his brow.

It was Tuesday afternoon of Blue Bottle's sprint. Sunlight made rectangles on the carpet. Somewhere on the street below, a car honked. And there, in the middle of the sprint room, on a coffee table, was the source of the team's consternation: a stack of paper, a dozen clipboards, and a paper cup filled with black pens.

Somebody cleared his throat. It was Byard Duncan, Blue Bottle's communications manager. As everyone turned, he cracked a sheepish smile.

"So . . . ," he said. "What if I can't draw?"

On Tuesday afternoon, it's time to come up with solutions. But there will be no brainstorming; no shouting over one another; no deferring judgment so wacky ideas can flourish. Instead, you'll work individually, take your time, and sketch.

Even though we're total tech nerds, we're believers in the importance of starting on paper. It's a great equalizer. Everyone can write words, draw boxes, and express his or her ideas with the same clarity. If you can't draw (or rather, if you *think* you can't draw), don't freak out. Plenty of people worry about putting pen to paper, but anybody—absolutely anybody—can sketch a great solution.

To show you what we're talking about, let's take a look at one of the sketches that came out of Blue Bottle Coffee's sprint—a solution called "The Mind Reader." Each sticky note represents one page on Blue Bottle's website.

The big idea behind "The Mind Reader" was to organize the online store the same way a barista might talk with a customer. As you can see in the three frames, this solution leads with a welcome, then asks how the customer prepares coffee at home, before offering recommendations and a brewing guide. There's a lot of complexity to the idea, but the drawing itself was straightforward: mostly boxes and text, the kind of thing anyone can draw.

Later in the week, the team made a realistic prototype based on "The Mind Reader," with details filled in from some of the other sketches. The prototype is on page 106.

On Friday, when shown to real customers, "The Mind Reader" was remarkably effective. Customers grew confident in the quality of the coffee as they clicked through the website. They found beans they wanted to order. They described the prototype as "way better" than competing retailers and mentioned that "clearly, these people know coffee." It was the big winner of Friday's test, and it became the foundation for Blue Bottle's new website.

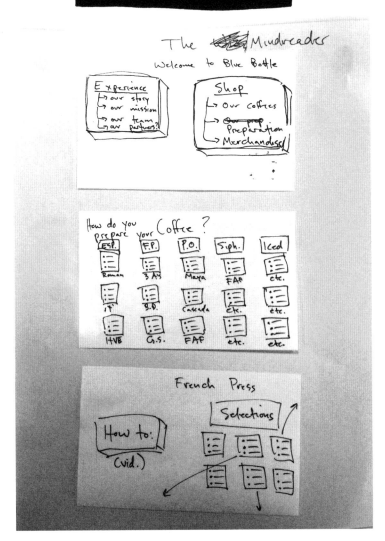

A solution from Blue Bottle Coffee's sprint. Each sticky note represents one screen.

The Mind Reader — Prototype

"Welcome" "How do you make coffee?" Recommendation

So, who sketched that solution? It wasn't a designer, an architect, or an illustrator. It was Byard Duncan, the Man Who Couldn't Draw.

See, Tuesday afternoon is about sketching, but more importantly, it's about solutions. When your team evaluates these sketches on Wednesday to decide which are best, and when you test your prototype on Friday, it will be the quality of the solutions that matters, not the artistry of the drawings from which they came.

The power of sketching

Imagine you've got a great idea. You've been thinking about it for weeks. You go to work, describe the idea to your teammates, and . . . they just stare at you. Maybe you aren't explaining it well. Maybe the timing isn't right. For whatever reason, they just can't picture it. Totally frustrating, right? It's about to get worse.

Now imagine your boss suggests an alternative idea. It just popped into his head, and you can tell right away that the idea isn't thought out and won't work. But all your teammates nod their heads! Maybe it's because the boss's idea is vague and each person is interpreting it in his or her own way. Maybe everyone is just supporting him because he's the boss. Either way, it's game over.

Okay, come back to reality. That was an imaginary scenario, but it's the sort of thing that happens when people make decisions about abstract ideas. Because abstract ideas lack concrete detail, it's easy for them to be undervalued (like your idea) or overvalued (like the boss's idea).

On Tuesday, we're not asking you to sketch because we think it's fun. We're asking you to sketch because we're convinced it's the fastest and easiest way to transform abstract ideas into concrete solutions. Once your ideas become concrete, they can be critically and fairly evaluated by the rest of the team—without any sales pitch. And, perhaps most important of all, sketching allows every person to develop those concrete ideas while working alone.

Work alone together

We know that individuals working alone generate better solutions than groups brainstorming out loud.* Working alone offers time to do research, find inspiration, and think about the problem. And the pressure of responsibility that comes with working alone often spurs us to our best work.

But working alone isn't easy. The individual has to not only solve the problem, but also *invent a strategy* for solving the problem. If you've ever sat down to work on a big project and wound up reading the news instead, you know how hard this work can be.

In our sprints, we work alone, but we follow specific steps to help everyone focus and make progress. When each person sketches alone, he or she will have time for deep thought. When the whole team works in parallel, they'll generate competing ideas, without the groupthink of a group brainstorm. You might call this method "work alone together."

---

*Jake learned the trouble with group brainstorms the hard way, but plenty of researchers have come to the same conclusion. One example is a study at Yale in 1958. Individuals competed with brainstorming groups to solve the same problem. The individuals dominated. They generated more solutions, and their solutions were independently judged to be higher quality and more original. In your face, group brainstorming! And yet . . . over half a century later, teams are still running group brainstorms. Perhaps it's because "brainstorm" is such a catchy name.

The sketches you create on Tuesday will become the fuel for the rest of the sprint. On Wednesday, you'll critique everyone's sketches and pick the best ones. On Thursday, you'll turn them into a prototype. And on Friday you'll test the ideas with customers. That's a lot of mileage out of a few drawings, and it might make you think we're expecting a work of genius straight out of Leonardo da Vinci's notebook. Not so. To put the power of the sketch in perspective, let's check out a few more solutions from the Blue Bottle sprint:

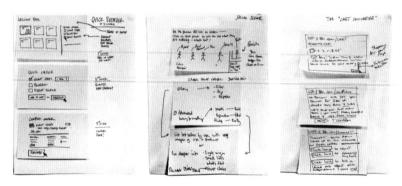

Three solution sketches from Blue Bottle Coffee's sprint.

As you can see, these sketches are detailed, but they're not works of art. Each sketch consists of words, boxes, and the occasional stick figure, drawn on normal printer paper and normal sticky notes with a normal pen.

Simple, right? So . . . Okay, you're all set. Go ahead and sketch a great solution!

We're just kidding. That blank sheet of paper always intimidates us. So, inspired by productivity expert David Allen, we break the process into steps. In his book *Getting Things Done*, Allen provides a smart strategy for daunting jobs. The secret, Allen writes, is not to think about the task as one monolithic effort (like "Pay taxes"), but instead to find the first small action needed to make progress (like "Collect tax paper-work") and go from there.

The four-step sketch

When Jake first started running sprints, he tried to re-create his own most successful work sessions. He was most effective when he took time to "boot up" by reviewing key information, started his design work on paper, considered multiple variations, and then took time to create a detailed solution. And, since Jake is a world-class procrastinator, he was also most effective when under a tight deadline.

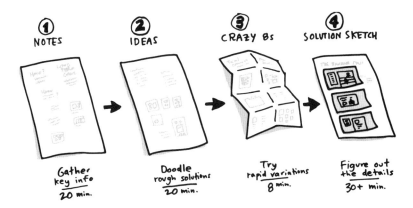

The four-step sketch contains each of these important elements. You'll start with twenty minutes to "boot up" by taking notes on the goals, opportunities, and inspiration you've collected around the room. Then you'll have another twenty minutes to write down rough ideas. Next, it's time to limber up and explore alternative ideas with a rapid sketching exercise called Crazy 8s. And finally, you'll take thirty minutes or more to draw your solution sketch—a single well-formed concept with all the details worked out.

1. Notes

This first step is super-easy. You and your team will walk around the room, look at the whiteboards, and take notes. These notes are a "greatest hits" from the past twenty-four hours of the sprint. They're a way to refresh your memory before you commit to a solution.

First, copy down the long-term goal. Next, look at the map, the How Might We questions, and the notes from your Lightning Demos. Write down anything that looks useful. Don't worry about coming up with any new ideas, and don't worry about being neat. These notes are for your eyes only.

Give your team twenty minutes to take notes. During this time, feel free to look up reference material on your laptop or phone. Sometimes people want to take a second look at something they saw in the morning's Lightning Demos or research some specific details from their company's own product or website. Whatever the purpose, this moment is a rare exception to the no-devices rule. And don't forget to reexamine old ideas. Remember, they're often the strongest solutions of all.

At the end of notes time, the team closes their laptops and phones. Take another three minutes to review what you wrote down. Circle the notes that stand out. They'll help you in the next step.

2. Ideas

Now that everyone has a pile of notes, it's time to switch into idea mode. In this step, each person will jot down rough ideas, filling a sheet of paper with doodles, sample headlines, diagrams, stick figures doing stuff—anything that gives form to his or her thoughts.

It doesn't matter if these ideas are messy or incomplete. Just like the notes, these pages won't be shared with the whole team. Think of them as a "scratch pad." And there's no wrong way to do it. As long as everyone is thinking and writing stuff on paper, you're on the golden path.

Your ideas might look like this, or they might not.
As long as you're writing things down, you're on the right track.

Take twenty minutes for idea generation. When you're finished, spend an extra three minutes to review and circle your favorite ideas. In the next step, you'll refine those promising elements.

3. Crazy 8s

Crazy 8s is a fast-paced exercise. Each person takes his or her strongest ideas and rapidly sketches eight variations in eight minutes. Crazy 8s forces you to push past your first reasonable solutions and make them better, or at least consider alternatives.

And before you get the wrong idea, the "crazy" in Crazy 8s refers to the pace, not the nature of the ideas. Forget about the traditional brainstorm advice to be goofy. We want you to focus on good ideas—the ones you believe will work and help you hit your goals—and use Crazy 8s to tweak and expand on those good ideas.

Each person begins Crazy 8s with a single sheet of letter-size paper. Fold the paper in half three times, so you have eight panels. Set a timer to sixty seconds. Hit "start" and begin sketching—you have sixty seconds per section, for a total of eight minutes to create eight miniature sketches. Go fast and be messy: As with the notes and ideas, Crazy 8s will not be shared with the team.

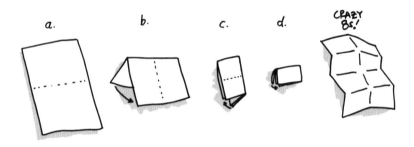

The exercise works best when you sketch several variations of the same idea. Take a favorite piece from your ideas sheet and ask yourself, "What would be another good way to do this?" Keep going until you can't think of any more variations, then look back at your ideas sheet, choose a new idea, and start riffing on it instead.

Crazy 8s is also a great writing exercise. If your idea contains words or marketing headlines or any other bits of text, you can use Crazy 8s to improve your phrasing. As you'll see in the next step, writing is often the most important component of the solution sketch.

Crazy 8s from the Blue Bottle Coffee sprint. The frames show experiments with phrasing ("hand pour coffee" vs. "pour over coffee"), navigation, and page layout.

Sometimes Crazy 8s leads to a revelation. You might come away with several new ways of looking at your ideas. Other times, it feels less productive. Sometimes that first idea really is the best idea. Either way, Crazy 8s helps you consider alternatives—and also serves as an excellent warm-up for the main event.

The GV team sketches with the founders of a startup called Move Loot.

4. Solution sketch

Remember how we kept saying, "Don't worry, nobody's going to look at this"? That time is over. The solution sketch is each person's best idea, put down on paper in detail. Each one is an opinionated hypothesis for how to solve the challenge at hand. These sketches *will* be looked at—and judged!—by the rest of the team. They need to be detailed, thought-out, and easy to understand.

Each sketch will be a three-panel storyboard drawn on sticky notes, showing what your customers see as they interact with your product or service. We like this storyboard format because products and services are more like movies than snapshots. Customers don't just appear in one freeze frame and then disappear in the next. Instead, they move through your solution like actors in a scene. Your solution has to move right along with them.

We usually use the three-panel format, but there are exceptions. Sometimes, a sprint will be focused on a single part of the customer experience. For instance: the home page, the front page of a medical report, the office lobby, or even the cover of a book. If your team has a "single scene" challenge, you might want to create a full-page sketch so you can show even more detail.

With either format, there are a few important rules to keep in mind:

1. Make it self-explanatory

On Wednesday morning, you'll post your sketch on the wall for everyone to see. It needs to explain itself. Think of this sketch as the first test for your idea. If no one can understand it in sketch form, it's not likely to do any better when it's polished.

2. Keep it anonymous

Don't put your name on your sketch, and be sure that everyone uses the same paper and the same black pens. On Wednesday, when you evaluate everyone's sketch, this anonymity will make it much easier to critique and choose the best ideas.

3. Ugly is okay

Your sketch does not have to be fancy (boxes, stick figures, and words are fine), but it does have to be detailed, thoughtful, and complete. Be as neat as you can, but don't worry if you're not much of an artist. However . . .

4. Words matter

We've used sprints with startups in all kinds of industries. One surprising constant: the importance of writing. Strong writing is especially necessary for software and marketing, where words often make up most of the screen. But choosing the right words is critical in every medium. So pay extra close attention to the writing in your sketch. Don't use "lorem ipsum" or draw those squiggly lines that mean "text will go here." That text will go a long way to explain your idea—so make it good and make it real!

5. Give it a catchy title

Since your name won't be on your sketch, give it a title. Later, these titles will help you keep track of the different solutions as you're reviewing and choosing. They're also a way to draw attention to the big idea in your solution sketch. (Byard Duncan titled his "The Mind Reader," partly for fun and partly to highlight the idea of making the perfect coffee match.)

Okay, get your paper ready. Refer to your notes, ideas, and Crazy 8s. Then uncap your pens, fasten your safety belts, and make sure your seat backs and tray tables are in their fully upright and locked positions. Your solution sketches are ready for takeoff.

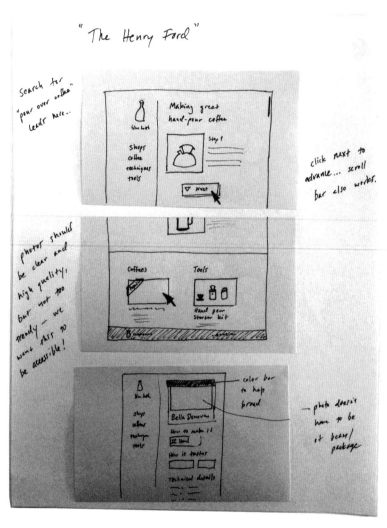

A solution sketch from the Blue Bottle Coffee sprint. To understand how this idea works, read the notes from top to bottom—as you would a comic book: In the top frame, the customer reads a how-to guide for brewing coffee. In the second frame, she clicks on a link to recommended coffee beans. In the third frame, she finds details about the beans.

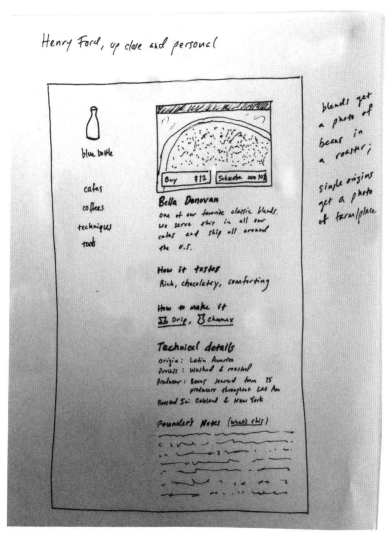

Henry Ford, up close and personal

blue bottle

cafes
coffees
techniques
tools

Buy $12   Subscribe save 10%

Bella Donovan
One of our favorite classic blends.
We serve this in all our
cafes and ship all around
the U.S.

How it tastes
Rich, chocolatey, comforting

How to make it
☑ Drip, ☐ chemex

Technical details
Origin: Latin America
Process: Washed & roasted
Producer: Beans sourced from 15
          producers throughout Lat Am
Roasted In: Oakland & New York

Founder's Notes (what's this)

blends get
a photo of
beans in
a roaster;

single origins
get a photo
of farm/place

Here's a single-sheet version of that same sketch from Blue Bottle's sprint. Instead of a storyboard, the entire page portrays one screen of the online store in detail.

Each person is responsible for creating one solution sketch. If a few folks get inspired and want to sketch more than one, that's okay, but don't overdo it. Each additional sketch means more work reviewing and narrowing down on Wednesday. Not only that, but we've noticed that the first batch tend to be the strongest and there are diminishing returns beyond ten to twelve solution sketches. Thirty minutes should be enough time for everyone to finish one sketch.

Once everybody is finished, put the solution sketches in a pile, but resist the urge to look at them. You'll only see them for the first time once, and you should save those fresh eyes for Wednesday.

FACILITATOR NOTES

Find Customers for Friday

On Monday or Tuesday, we start the process of finding customers for Friday's test. That means one person needs to do some extra work outside of the sprint. It takes all week—but only an hour or two a day—to screen, select, and recruit the best matches. Ideally, someone besides the Facilitator should take responsibility for recruiting, since the Facilitator will be busy enough as it is.

There are two ways to find the right customers for your test. If you have fairly easy-to-find customers, you'll use Craigslist. If you have hard-to-find customers, you'll use your network.

Recruit customers with Craigslist

Most of the time, to recruit people who exactly match our target customer, we use Craigslist. We know it sounds crazy, but it works. It's how we found perfect participants for our tests with Savioke and Blue Bottle Coffee—and dozens of other companies. The secret is to post a generic ad that will attract a broad audience, then link to a screener survey to narrow down to your target customers.

First, you'll write your generic ad. You want to be sure you don't reveal what you're testing or the kind of customer you're seeking. We offer a small stipend or token of appreciation—usually a $100 gift card—to pique the interest of potential customers. Post in the "et cetera jobs" with something like this:

TUESDAY

> **$100 customer research interviews on August 2 (San Francisco)**
>
> I'm scheduling 60-minute research interviews in San Francisco on Thursday, August 2. Selected participants who complete the interviews will receive $100 Amazon gift cards. Please complete this short questionnaire. <u>Click here.</u>

As you can see, this ad could be about anything—coffee, robots, coffee robots, whatever. A generic ad in a big city may attract hundreds of applicants, so with the right screener, you'll be able to find five people who fit your customer profile.

Write a screener survey

The screener survey is a simple questionnaire for interested people to fill out. You'll need to ask the right questions to find the right people. Start by writing down characteristics of the customers you want to test with, then translate those characteristics into something you can discover with your survey. Do the same thing for characteristics you want to exclude (for example, people with too much expertise in your industry).

Blue Bottle Coffee wanted to interview "coffee-drinking foodies." To find these customers, we used measurable criteria like: they drink at least one cup of coffee per day, they read food-related blogs and magazines, and they eat at restaurants at least once per week. We excluded people who didn't make coffee at home or drank coffee infrequently.

Next, write questions for every one of your criteria. It's important to write questions that don't reveal the "right" answers—some people will try to game the survey just so they can get the gift card. For example, rather than asking people whether they go to restaurants, ask: "In a typical week, how many times do you eat out?" Instead of asking if applicants read food blogs, try something like this: "Do you regularly read blogs or magazines dedicated to any of the following topics?

- ❏ Sports
- ❏ Food
- ❏ News
- ❏ Coffee
- ❏ Cocktails
- ❏ Parenting
- ❏ Gardening
- ❏ Cars

In each of these examples, we had a "right" answer in mind, but there was no way that the person filling out the survey could predict what it was.

After you've turned your criteria into questions, create your survey. We always use Google Forms—it's easy to set up, and the responses go right into a Google spreadsheet that you can sort and filter.

Once your screener survey is ready and your ad is live on Craigslist, the responses will start rolling in. Look through the survey results and pick out customers who match your criteria. By Wednesday afternoon, you can start getting in touch with people and scheduling your interviews for Friday.

Craigslist works surprisingly well for finding customers who aren't familiar with your company. But what about existing customers or "hard-to-find" professionals with uncommon jobs? You'll need a different strategy.

Recruit customers through your network

Finding existing customers is generally pretty easy. You probably already have the means to reach them—consider email newsletters, in-store posters, Twitter, Facebook, or even your own website.

The hard-to-find customers are not actually so hard to find, either. Here's why: If you're an oncology company, you probably know some oncologists. If you're working in finance, you probably know other people who work in finance. And so on. Your sales or business-development teams can help you get in touch. And if that fails, you can reach out to professional associations, community groups, student groups, or your personal network. When we interviewed restaurant managers for a sprint back in 2011, we got in touch with the membership director of a local restaurant association.

Whether you're seeking out hard-to-find customers, existing customers, or recruiting a broad audience on Craigslist, there's one part of the process that shouldn't change. Make sure potential interview candidates match your screening criteria. With only five interviews, it's important to talk to the right people.

The entire sprint depends on getting good data in Friday's test, so whoever takes charge of recruiting your customers should take the job seriously. Even though this recruiting happens behind the scenes, it's as important as the team activities. For a sample screening survey and other online resources, take a look at thesprintbook.com.

Wednesday

By Wednesday morning, you and your team will have a stack of solutions. That's great, but it's also a problem. You can't prototype and test them all—you need one solid plan. In the morning, you'll critique each solution, and decide which ones have the best chance of achieving your long-term goal. Then, in the afternoon, you'll take the winning scenes from your sketches and weave them into a storyboard: a step-by-step plan for your prototype.

10

Decide

You know those meetings. The ones that go on and on, wandering off on tangents, burning up time and energy. The ones that end in a decision nobody's happy about—or worse, end without any decision at all. We're not anthropologists, but we have observed (and engaged in) a lot of human behavior in the office environment. Left to our own devices, we humans tend to debate this way:

Okay, we're exaggerating, but not that much. You might recognize this kind of back-and-forth. Someone comes up with a solution, the group critiques it, someone tries to explain the details, and then someone *else* has a new idea:

These discussions are frustrating, because humans have limited short-term memory and limited energy for decision-making. When we jump from option to option, it's difficult to hold important details in our heads. On the other hand, when we debate one idea for too long, we get worn out—like a judge at a baking contest who fills up on apple pie before tasting anything else.

Normally, if we want the benefit of everyone's perspective, we're forced to endure these slogs. But not in a sprint. We've structured Wednesday to do one thing at a time—and do it well. We'll evaluate solutions all at once, critique all at once, and then make a decision all at once. Kind of like this:

Your goal for Wednesday morning is to decide which solutions to prototype. Our motto for these decisions is "unnatural but efficient." Instead of meandering, your team's conversations will follow a script. This structure is socially awkward, but logical—if you feel like Spock from *Star Trek*, you're doing it right. It's all designed to get the most out of the team's expertise, accommodate for our human strengths and shortcomings, and make it as easy as possible to come to a great decision.

To show you what Wednesday looks like, we'd like to introduce you to another startup. This company makes business software, but they didn't start out that way. In fact, their first product was a video game called *Glitch*.

Glitch was unusual: a multiplayer game with no combat. Instead of fighting, the game encouraged players to collaborate, solve problems, and chat together in groups. Unfortunately—say what you will about society—this unusual game with its emphasis on good behavior never caught on with a big audience.

When it became obvious that *Glitch* wasn't going to be a hit, the company did something strange. Instead of making a different game or closing down, they shifted their efforts to a side project: a messaging system they had originally built for their own use. The startup's founder, Stewart Butterfield, had a hunch that this messaging system could be useful to other companies, too. So they launched it to the public, and named it Slack.

Technology companies went bonkers for Slack. A year after launch, more than 500,000 people on more than 60,000 teams used Slack every single day. For workplace software, this kind of growth was unheard of. When Slack announced they were the fastest growing business app of all time, the press agreed.

Slack was growing fast, but—like any team—they had challenges. One of those challenges was maintaining their rapid growth. Many of the teams adopting Slack were at tech companies, which are often more willing to try new software. But there were only so many tech companies in the world. To keep expanding, Slack needed to get better at explaining their product to all kinds of businesses. It was a tricky problem. On the surface, Slack was simple: a messaging app for the workplace. But under the surface, the story was more complicated.

Slack had become so popular because it changed the way teams functioned. Teams started by using the service to send instant messages to one another, and then often abandoned email in favor of it. But Slack wasn't just for one-to-one messages. When a team used Slack, all of its employees were in a chat room, so they could communicate as a group. Soon, Slack replaced check-in meetings and phone calls. Teams used it to manage projects and stay up to speed on what the whole company was doing. They connected other software and services to Slack, so that everything was in one place. Slack became the hub for all of their work, and that efficiency and connectedness somehow made work feel good. As a reporter for the *New York Times*—one of the workplaces that had adopted Slack—put it, "I have a feeling of intimacy with coworkers on the other side of the country that is almost fun. That's a big deal, for a job."

That whole story of Slack—how it provided a service that was familiar, but different and somehow better . . . Well, that story was *really* difficult to explain, especially as Slack expanded to new audiences.

Merci Grace, a product manager new to the company, was in charge of solving this problem. It was her team's job to figure out how to explain Slack to potential customers. Merci decided to start with a sprint, and since GV was an investor in Slack, she invited us to join.

The sprint team included Merci, two designers, an engineer, and a marketer, along with a few of us from GV. On Wednesday morning, everything was right on schedule. There were about a dozen solution sketches, all stuck to the glass walls with blue masking tape.

We walked around the room in silence, seeing one another's ideas for the first time. One sketch featured a case study of a well-known company using Slack, one sketch had an animated video, and one introduced the software with a guided tour. Each of the dozen ideas for explaining Slack was different, and each had potential. It would be a difficult decision.

Luckily, we didn't have to make any choices right away. Instead, we placed dot stickers beside the parts of ideas we found interesting. After a few minutes, there were clusters of dots on almost every sketch. When we were done with our silent review, we gathered into a group and discussed the sketches, one at a time. We kept the conversations short by focusing on the clusters of dots—and by using a timer.

It took just under an hour to review all of the sketches. When we were done, everyone took a pink dot sticker to cast his or her final vote. After a few minutes of deliberation, each person silently placed the sticker on the sketch he or she wanted to prototype and test.

After a short discussion, the decision was turned over to Merci, the Decider, and Stewart—who, as CEO, made a cameo appearance to share his opinion. They looked at the pink stickers, took a moment to think, and placed their own "supervotes." And with that—with no meandering debate and no sales pitches—the decision was made.

In the Slack sprint, there were about a dozen different solutions for explaining the product to new customers. Each person believed his or her own idea could work. And each person could have spent an hour explaining why. But if we had spent an hour discussing each idea, the whole day could have gone by without any clear conclusion.

Instead, we used the sprint process to reshape that open-ended discussion into efficient critique and decision-making. By the end of the morning, we knew which ideas we wanted to test.

The sticky decision

We've spent years optimizing our sprint decisions to be as efficient as possible. We ended up with a five-step process—and coincidentally, every step involves something sticky:

1. **Art museum:** Put the solution sketches on the wall with masking tape.
2. **Heat map:** Look at all the solutions in silence, and use dot stickers to mark interesting parts.
3. **Speed critique:** Quickly discuss the highlights of each solution, and use sticky notes to capture big ideas.
4. **Straw poll:** Each person chooses one solution, and votes for it with a dot sticker.
5. **Supervote:** The Decider makes the final decision, with— you guessed it—more stickers.

This sticky stuff isn't a gimmick. The dot stickers let us form and express our opinions without lengthy debate, and the sticky notes allow us to record big ideas without relying on our short-term memory. (For a complete sprint shopping list, see the checklists at the end of the book.)

Of course, there are more reasons for all of these steps, but we'll explain those as we go. Here's how the Sticky Decision works:

1. Art museum

The first step is simple. When you arrive on Wednesday morning, nobody has seen the solution sketches yet. We want everybody to take a good long look at each one, so we stole an idea from the Louvre Museum in Paris: hang them on the wall.

Specifically, use masking tape to stick the sketches on a wall. Space them out in one long row, just like the paintings in a museum. This spacing allows the team to spread out and take their time examining each sketch without crowding. It's also a good idea to place the sketches in roughly chronological order, following the storyboard.

2. Heat map

Naturally, every person should have a fair opportunity to present his or her solution and explain the rationale behind it. Well . . . that may be natural, but you're not going to do it.

Explaining ideas has all kinds of downsides. If someone makes a compelling case for his or her idea or is a bit more charismatic, your opinion will be skewed. If you associate the idea with its creator ("Jamie always has great ideas"), your opinion will be skewed. Even just by knowing *what the idea is about,* your opinion will be skewed.

It's not hard for creators to make great arguments for their mediocre ideas, or give great explanations for their indecipherable ideas. But in the real world, the creators won't be there to give sales pitches and clues. In the real world, the ideas will have to stand on their own. If they're confusing to the experts in a sprint, chances are good they'll be confusing to customers.

The heat map exercise ensures you make the most of your first, uninformed look at the sketches. So before the team begins looking, hand everyone a bunch of small dot stickers (twenty to thirty dots each). Then each person follows these steps:

1. Don't talk.
2. Look at a solution sketch.
3. Put dot stickers beside the parts you like (if any).
4. Put two or three dots on the most exciting ideas.
5. If you have a concern or question, write it on a sticky note and place it below the sketch.
6. Move on to the next sketch, and repeat.

There are no limits or rules for these dots. If people want to put dots on their own sketch, they should. If people run out of dots, give them more. By the end, you'll have something like this:

Heat map: Clusters of dots mark standout ideas

Questions and concerns go below

Together, all those dots create a "heat map" on top of the sketches—kind of like a heat map of the weather—showing which ideas the group finds intriguing. It's a simple activity, but as you'll see over the coming pages, this heat map forms the foundation for the Sticky Decision.

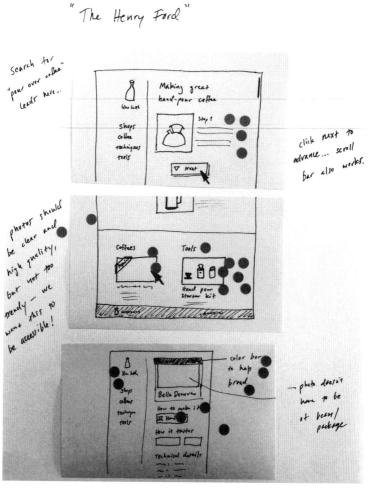

A solution sketch with heat map dots.

Because this process is quick, it's possible to load all of the sketches into short-term memory at once. And since there are unlimited stickers, you and your team won't use up much of your decision-making energy. The heat map is both a useful way to spot standout ideas *and* a great way to get your brain warmed up for a decision.

But the heat map has limitations. It can't tell you *why* people liked an idea, and if you don't understand the sketcher's intent, the heat map can't explain it to you. To find out, you need to discuss the sketches with the team. Of course, that means talking out loud, something we've mostly avoided since Tuesday morning. Hopefully you haven't forgotten how to do it.

Talking out loud is risky. Humans are social animals, and when our natural impulses to discuss and debate take over, time disappears. We don't want to tax anyone's short-term memory, or waste precious sprint time. So in the next step, your team will talk out loud—but you'll follow a script.

3. Speed critique

In the speed critique, you and your team will discuss each solution sketch and make note of standout ideas. The conversation will follow a structure—and a time limit. The first time you do it, it might feel uncomfortable and rushed, and it might be hard to keep track of all the steps (when in doubt, use a checklist from the back of the book). But it won't take long to get the hang of it. Once you do, your team will have a powerful tool for analyzing ideas, and you may find yourselves using it in other meetings.

During the speed critique, the Facilitator is going to be very busy, so someone needs to volunteer to help by being the Scribe. As you review the sketches on the wall, the Scribe will write down standout ideas on sticky notes. The Scribe's notes serve several purposes. The notes give everyone a common vocabulary to describe solutions. They help everyone on the team to feel heard, which speeds up the discussion. And they organize the team's observations, making it easier to place your votes in the next step.

Here's how the speed critique works:

1. **Gather** around a solution sketch.
2. **Set a timer for three minutes**.
3. **The Facilitator narrates** the sketch. ("Here it looks like a customer is clicking to play a video, and then clicking over to the details page . . .")
4. **The Facilitator calls out standout ideas** that have clusters of stickers by them. ("Lots of dots by the animated video . . .")
5. **The team calls out standout ideas** that the Facilitator missed.
6. **The Scribe writes standout ideas on sticky notes** and sticks them above the sketch. Give each idea a simple name, like "Animated Video" or "One-Step Signup."
7. **Review concerns and questions**.
8. **The creator of the sketch remains silent until the end**. ("Creator, reveal your identity and tell us what we missed!")
9. **The creator explains any missed ideas** that the team failed to spot, and answers any questions.
10. Move to the next sketch and repeat.

That's right—the proud inventor of the solution in the spotlight doesn't get to speak up until the end of the critique. This unusual practice saves time, removes redundancy, and allows for the most honest discussion. (If the inventor pitched his or her idea, the rest of the team would have a harder time being critical or negative.)

Try to keep each review to three minutes, but be a little flexible. If a sketch has a lot of good ideas, take a couple of extra minutes to capture them all. On the other hand, if a sketch has very few dots, and the creator doesn't have a compelling explanation, do everyone a favor and move on quickly. Nothing is gained by tearing apart a sketch nobody likes.

Remember that all you're trying to accomplish in the speed critique is to create a record of promising ideas. You don't need to debate whether something should be included in the prototype; that will come later. You shouldn't try to come up with new ideas on the spot. Just write down what stands out about each solution.

By the end of the speed critique, everyone will understand all of the promising ideas and details. You'll also have a nice tangible record of the discussion on the wall, like this:

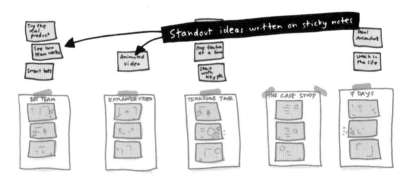

If you're the Facilitator, the speed critique will require you to think on your feet and keep the group moving. You're both narrator and referee, but the process should be fun. After all, the solutions will be interesting, and since the discussion focuses on the best ideas, the tone will be positive.

4. Straw poll

In case you're not a politics nerd, a straw poll is a nonbinding vote used to gauge a group's opinion (like holding up a piece of straw to see which way the wind is blowing). In your sprint, the straw poll serves the same purpose. It's a quick way for the whole team to express their opinions. These votes aren't binding. Instead, think of the straw poll as a way to give your Decider some advice. It's a straightforward exercise:

1. **Give everyone one vote** (represented by a big dot sticker—we like pink).
2. Remind everyone of the **long-term goal** and **sprint questions**.
3. Remind everyone to **err on the side of risky ideas** with big potential.
4. **Set a timer for ten minutes.**
5. **Each person privately writes down his or her choice.** It could be a whole sketch, or just one idea in a sketch.
6. When time is up, or when everyone is finished, **place the votes on the sketches.**
7. **Each person briefly explains his or her vote** (only spend about one minute per person).

There are plenty of clues to assist your voting. In the last chapter, we asked you to give a catchy name to each solution. During the straw poll, those names—along with the heat map and the sticky notes from the speed critique—make it easier to compare and weigh the options.

We've talked a lot about human limitations, but this kind of decision is one place where the brain shines. Each person in the room has special expertise and years of accumulated wisdom. With the speed critique loaded into short-term memory, those sophisticated brains can focus on just one task. No managing a conversation, no articulating your opinions, no trying to remember what that sketch was all about. Just apply your expertise and make an informed decision. Brains are great at that.

For a few minutes, the team silently will consider where to vote. And then ... that's it: The stickers go up.

Afterward, each person will give a brief explanation of his or her vote. The Decider should listen to these explanations—because all decision-making authority is about to be turned over to her.

Make honest decisions

Sometimes when people work together in groups, they start to worry about consensus and try to make decisions that everybody will approve—mostly out of good nature and a desire for group cohesion, and perhaps in part because democracy feels good. Well, democracy is a fine system for governing nations, but it has no place in your sprint.

Earlier in the book, we told you about our mistake with SquidCo: not including the Decider in the sprint. A few weeks later, we had a sprint with a company we'll call OstrichCo.* We had learned our lesson about Deciders, so OstrichCo's founder and CEO, Oscar, joined us for the entire sprint.

On Wednesday, it came time for OstrichCo to choose ideas. "You know, this is something we should all decide together," said Oscar. "We're a team." Everybody felt great, and everybody voted. The solution the team chose wasn't Oscar's favorite, but it performed well in Friday's test. The sprint was a success. Or so we thought, until we talked to Oscar a couple of weeks later.

---

*Names and identifying details changed to protect the innocent.

"Yeah . . ." Oscar rubbed the back of his head. He looked bashful. "I thought about it some more and, uh . . . decided to go in another direction."

"Let me guess," said John. "You went with your favorite idea from the sprint."

"Well," said Oscar. "Yeah."

During the sprint, Oscar had succumbed to camaraderie. He wanted to let the team make the decision. But the idea the team chose wasn't the idea Oscar was most excited about. Later, after the prototyping and testing were over, he reverted to his normal method of decision-making—and now OstrichCo was committed to Oscar's untested idea.

So who screwed up here? It wasn't just Oscar. It was all of us in the sprint, because we let him cede his authority. The lesson of OstrichCo is to **make honest decisions**. You brought your Decider into the sprint room for a reason, and right now, more than at any other moment, you need the Decider to do her job.

Of course, being the Decider isn't easy. Many of the startup CEOs we talk to feel the pressure of having to make the right decisions for their companies and teams. In the sprint, those Deciders get plenty of decision-making assistance. Between the detailed sketches, the collective notes, and the just-completed straw poll, the Deciders should have everything they need.

5. Supervote

The supervote is the ultimate decision. Each Decider will get three special votes (with the Decider's initials on them!), and whatever they vote for is what your team will prototype and test.

Deciders can choose ideas that were popular in the straw poll. Or they can choose to ignore the straw poll. They can spread out their votes, or put them all in one place. Basically, the Deciders can do whatever the heck they want.

The Decider's supervote stickers

What everybody else gets

All the same, it's a good idea to remind the Decider of the long-term goal and the sprint questions (which should still be on one of your whiteboards!). Finally, when the Decider has placed her votes, the hardest choice of the week is complete. It'll look something like this:

Supervotes

The sketches with supervotes on them (even just one!) are the winners. You'll plan your prototype around those ideas and put them to the test on Friday. We like to rearrange the sketches on the wall, so that the supervote winners are all together, like this:

Ideas with supervotes are the foundation for your prototype.

WINNERS

MAYBE LATERS

The sketches that didn't get any supervotes aren't winners, but they aren't losers either. They're "maybe-laters." You might incorporate them when you plan your prototype on Wednesday afternoon, or perhaps you'll use them in your next sprint.

It's important to note that this decision-making process isn't perfect. Sometimes, Deciders screw up. Sometimes, good ideas don't get selected (at least, not in the first sprint). But the "sticky decision"—if not perfect—is pretty good and very speedy. That speed helps with the sprint's larger goal: getting real world data from Friday's test. Ultimately, it will be that data that leads to the best decisions of all.

After your team has organized the winning solutions, everyone will probably feel relieved—after all, the biggest decision of the sprint has been made. Everyone will have had a chance to be heard, and everyone will understand how the decision was reached. On top of that relief, it's exciting to identify and see the building blocks of your prototype.

But there is one more hitch. Since each Decider gets three votes, and there are sometimes two Deciders, there is bound to be more than one winning sketch. So what do you do if those winning sketches conflict with one another? What do you do if those ideas can't coexist in the same prototype? In the next chapter, you'll find out.

11

Rumble

Stewart Butterfield, Slack's founder and CEO, studied a sketch called "Bot Team." It showed a new customer trying out Slack by talking to a team of "bots"—computer-controlled characters who could send messages and reply to simple questions. Stewart nodded and scratched his stubbly chin. Then he stuck his final pink sticker on the page, and the supervote was complete.

Stewart told us he had a hunch about "Bot Team." Potential customers had difficulty imagining what it would be like to use Slack at work. With the simulation provided by "Bot Team," Stewart predicted those customers would get it right away.

Stewart is a repeat entrepreneur who is known for having really good hunches. He'd followed a hunch to create Slack after the game *Glitch* failed to catch on. A decade earlier, he'd followed a hunch to create the photo sharing service Flickr. Needless to say, when Stewart said he had a hunch about the sketch called "Bot Team," we listened. Still,

143

Merci, the product manager, worried that the fake team might confuse customers. Not only that, she estimated that the engineering required to implement it properly could take four to six months.

Merci had credibility, too. She was an experienced entrepreneur, having started a software company of her own before joining Slack. And as head of the project, she was also a Decider for the sprint. Her supervotes had gone to another sketch: "The Tenacious Tour," a solution that explained Slack's interface step-by-step.

This supervote conflict posed a problem, because we couldn't figure out how to put "Bot Team" and "The Tenacious Tour" together in the same prototype. It would be way too much explanation for one website. With two great ideas and no way to combine them, there was only one sensible course of action. It was time for a Rumble.

On Wednesday morning, your team will make a Sticky Decision to narrow down to the most promising sketches. But what if, like Slack, you end up with two (or even three) winning sketches that can't coexist? Since Deciders get three supervotes, this kind of conflict happens all the time. It might sound like a problem, but actually it's a bonanza.

When you have two good, conflicting ideas, you don't have to choose between them at all. Instead, you can prototype both, and in Friday's test, you'll be able to see how each one fares with your customers. Your prototypes will battle head-to-head, like professional wrestlers whacking each other with folding chairs. We call this kind of test a Rumble.

A Rumble allows your team to explore multiple options at once. For Slack, it meant building two prototypes: one for "The Tenacious Tour" and one for "Bot Team." Merci and Stewart didn't have to argue, or compromise on a watered-down solution. With a sprint, they could get data in just five days—before they made a commitment. (Later in this book, we'll tell you whose hunch was correct.)

Of course, it doesn't always make sense to do a Rumble. Sometimes, there's just one winning sketch. Sometimes, there are many winners, but they all fit together. Savioke's winning solutions for their robot personality—sound effects, survey, and happy dance—could all coexist in one prototype. Which was lucky, because we only had one robot.

If you think you can combine your winning sketches into one product, don't bother with a Rumble. Instead, put them together into your best shot at solving the problem. This all-in-one approach has advantages, too. Your prototype will be longer and more detailed.

Rumble or all-in-one

If you have more than one winning solution, involve the whole team in a short discussion about whether to do a Rumble or combine the winners into a single prototype. Typically, this decision about format is easy. If it's not, you can always ask the Decider to make the call.

Now, if you decide to do a Rumble, you'll have one more small problem. If you show your customers two prototypes of the same product, you risk sounding like an optometrist: "Which version do you prefer? A, or B? A? Or B?"*

Luckily, the resolution to this murky situation is easy, and even fun: You get to create some fake brands. Once your prototypes have their own distinct names and look, customers will be able to tell them apart.

In Slack's sprint, we decided to use the Slack brand for one prototype, but we needed a fake name for the other one. We knew customers wouldn't take a prototype seriously if it had a name like "Acme" or "Clown Pants." It had to sound like a realistic competitor to Slack. After thinking up a few options, the team chose "Gather" for the second prototype. That name was perfect: It wasn't a real product, but it sounded like it could be.

---

* Not that there's anything wrong with optometrists. We love optometrists.

WEDNESDAY

Blue Bottle Coffee faced a similar challenge when they tested different ideas for their online store. They needed fake brand names that sounded like real coffee companies, and they came up with "Linden Alley Coffee," "Telescope Coffee," and "Potting Shed Coffee."

Inventing fake brands is fun, but it's also a potential time waster. To keep the process short, we use an all-purpose brainstorm substitute that we call Note-and-Vote. Here's how it works:

Note-and-Vote

Throughout the sprint, you'll have times when you need to gather information or ideas from the group and then make a decision. The Note-and-Vote is a shortcut. It only takes about ten minutes, and it works great for everything from fake brand names to deciding where to get lunch.

1. Give each team member a piece of **paper and a pen.**

2. Everyone takes **three minutes and quietly writes down ideas.**

3. Everyone takes **two minutes to self-edit** his or her list down to the best two or three ideas.

4. Write each person's **top ideas on the whiteboard.** In a sprint with seven people, you'll have roughly fifteen to twenty ideas in all.

5. Everyone takes **two minutes and quietly chooses his or her favorite idea** from the whiteboard.

6. Going around the room, **each person calls out his or her favorite.** For each "vote," draw a dot next to the chosen idea on the whiteboard.

7. **The Decider makes the final decision.** As always, she can choose to follow the votes or not.

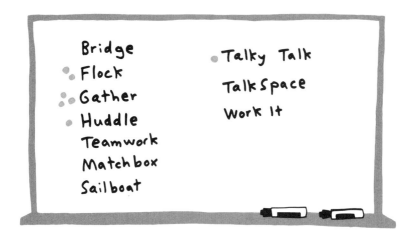

By lunchtime on Wednesday, you will have decided which sketches have the best chance of answering your sprint questions and helping you reach your long-term goal. You'll also decide whether to combine those winning ideas into one prototype or build two or three and test them in a Rumble. Next, it's time to turn all these decisions into a plan of action so you can finish your prototype in time for Friday's test.

12

Storyboard .

By Wednesday afternoon, you'll be able to feel Friday's test with customers looming ahead. Because of the short timeline, it's tempting to jump into prototyping as soon as you've selected your winning ideas. But if you start prototyping without a plan, you'll get bogged down by small, unanswered questions. Pieces won't fit together, and your prototype could fall apart.

On Wednesday afternoon, you'll answer those small questions and make a plan. Specifically, you'll take the winning sketches and string them together into a storyboard. This will be similar to the three-panel storyboards you sketched on Tuesday, but it will be longer: about ten to fifteen panels, all tightly connected into one cohesive story.

This kind of long-form storyboarding is a common practice in movie production. Pixar, the film studio behind movies like *Toy Story* and *The Incredibles*, spends months getting their storyboards right before committing to animation. For Pixar, the up-front effort makes sense: It's much easier to change storyboards than to re-render animation or re-record voice tracks with super-famous actors.

Sprints have a shorter timeline and smaller scale than a Pixar production. But storyboarding is still worthwhile. You'll use your storyboard to imagine your finished prototype, so you can spot problems and points of confusion before the prototype is built. By taking care of those decisions up front, you'll be free to focus on Thursday.

Slack's storyboard showed how their prototype would work, following the customers as they read about the two products (Slack and Gather) in a news article, then clicked through to the websites, and, hopefully, signed up for the service.

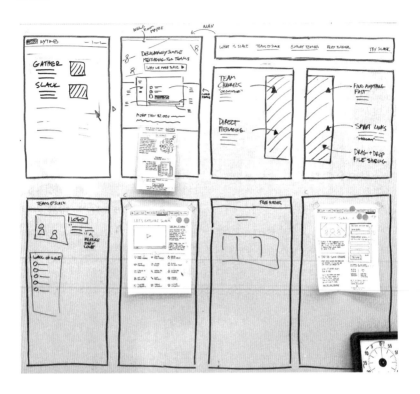

At a glance, this storyboard might look like the world's most boring (and poorly drawn) comic strip. But for the Slack team, it was a masterpiece. The storyboard contained all of our best ideas, stuck together in a story we could all understand, and we hoped it would make sense to customers, too. When we looked at the whiteboard, we saw this:

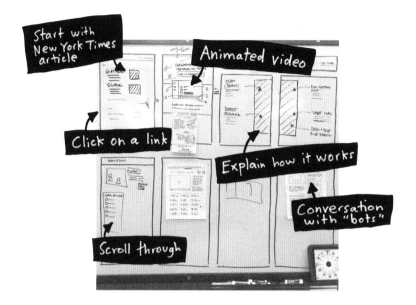

When you're finished, your storyboard will make just as much sense to your team as Slack's storyboard did to them. Next, we'll dive right in and talk about how to make one, and as we go, we'll show you how Slack put theirs together.

First of all, somebody needs to be the storyboard "artist." We put the word "artist" in quotes because the job doesn't require artistic talent. In this case, the "artist" is just someone willing to write on the whiteboard a lot. (It might be another good time to give the Facilitator a break.)

Draw a grid

First, you need a big grid with around fifteen frames. **Draw a bunch of boxes on an empty whiteboard**, each about the size of two sheets of paper. If you have a hard time drawing long straight lines (and who doesn't), use masking tape instead of a marker.

You'll start drawing your storyboard in the top left box of the grid. This frame will be the first moment that customers experience on Friday. So . . . what should it be? What's the best opening scene for your prototype?

If you get it right, the opening scene will boost the quality of your test. The right context can help customers forget they're trying a prototype and react to your product in a natural way—just as if they had come across it on their own. If you're prototyping an app, start in the App Store. If you're prototyping a new cereal box, start on a grocery shelf. And if you're prototyping business communication software?

In real life, Slack was getting lots of great press. Many of their new customers discovered the service by reading an article about it. So Merci suggested we use a fake *New York Times* article for our opening scene. The article could be about "new trends in office software"—giving us the perfect opportunity to introduce our two prototypes, Slack and Gather. Here's how we drew it on the storyboard:

The fake news article is a useful opening scene. We used the same method in our sprint with Blue Bottle, when we opened with a (fake) *New York Times* article about three (fake) up-and-coming coffee companies.

But there are lots of ways to open your storyboard. Flatiron Health wondered if existing users of their software would change their workflow for a new clinical-trial tool. A news article wouldn't have made much sense. Instead, Flatiron's opening scene was an email inbox—the place research coordinators would receive notifications from the new system. For Savioke, the opening scene was checking in to a hotel and forgetting a toothbrush. The trick is to take one or two steps upstream from the beginning of the actual solution you want to test.

Choose an opening scene

How do customers find out your company exists? Where are they and what are they doing just before they use your product? Our favorite opening scenes are simple:

- **Web search** with your website nestled among the results
- **Magazine** with an advertisement for your service
- **Store shelf** with your product sitting beside its competitors
- **App Store** with your app in it
- **News article** that mentions your service, and possibly some competitors
- **Facebook** or **Twitter** feed with your product shared among the other posts

There are other possible opening scenes. Your prototype might begin with an everyday routine: a doctor's folder of paper reports, an engineer's email inbox, or a teacher's classroom newsletter. If you're testing a new kind of store, you might start the moment people enter the front door.

It's almost always a good idea to **present your solution alongside the competition.** As a matter of fact, you can ask customers to test out your competitors' products on Friday right alongside your own prototype.

Once you choose an opening scene, you only have nine hundred more decisions to make before you're done with your storyboard. Just kidding . . . kind of.

Storyboarding is a simple process, with a ton of tiny decisions along the way. Those tiny decisions can be tiring, but remember—you're doing your future self a favor. Every decision you make now is something you won't have to think about when you build your prototypes.

Fill out the storyboard

Once you've selected an opening scene, the storyboard "artist" should draw it in the first frame (the "artist" will be standing at the whiteboard while everyone else gathers around). From there, you'll build out your story, one frame at a time, just like a comic book. As you go, you'll discuss each step as a team.

Whenever possible, use the sticky notes from your winning sketches and stick them onto the whiteboard. When you come to a gap—a step in the story not already illustrated by one of the solution sketches—don't fill it in unless it's critical to testing your idea. It's okay if some parts of your prototype don't work. You can have buttons that don't function and menu items that are unavailable. Surprisingly, these "dead ends" are generally easy for customers to ignore in Friday's test.

If you decide the gap does need to be filled, try to use something from your "maybe-later" sketches, or from your existing product. Avoid inventing a new solution on the spot. Coming up with ideas on Wednesday afternoon isn't a good use of time or effort. You will have to do some drawing, of course: filling in gaps when necessary and expanding on the winning sketches so that your prototype will be a believable story. Remember that the drawing doesn't have to be fancy. If the scene happens on screen, draw buttons and words and a little arrow clicking. If the scene happens in real life, draw stick figures and speech bubbles.

Making your storyboard will likely take up the entire afternoon. To make sure you finish by 5 p.m., follow these guidelines:

Work with what you have.

Resist inventing new ideas and just work with the good ideas you already came up with.

Don't write together.

Your storyboard should include rough headlines and important phrases, but don't try to perfect your writing as a group. Group copywriting is a recipe for bland, meandering junk, not to mention lots of wasted time. Instead, use the writing from your solution sketches, or just leave it until Thursday.

Include just enough detail.

Put enough detail in your storyboard so that nobody has to ask questions like "What happens next?" or "What goes here?" when they are prototyping on Thursday. But don't get too specific. You don't need to perfect every frame or figure out every nuance. It's okay to say: "Whoever builds this tomorrow can decide that detail." And then move on.

The Decider decides.

Storyboarding is difficult because you already spent a lot of your limited decision-making energy in the morning. To make it easier, continue to rely on the Decider. In the Slack sprint, Braden was the "artist" drawing the storyboard, but Merci made the decisions. It was extra work for her, but it kept us fast and opinionated.

You won't be able to fit in every good idea and still have a storyboard that makes sense. And you can't spend all day arguing about what to include. The Decider can ask for advice or defer to experts for some parts—but don't dissolve back into a democracy.

When in doubt, take risks.

Sometimes you can't fit everything in. Remember that the sprint is great for testing risky solutions that might have a huge payoff. So you'll have to reverse the way you would normally prioritize. If a small fix is so good and low-risk that you're already planning to build it next week, then seeing it in a prototype won't teach you much. Skip those easy wins in favor of big, bold bets.

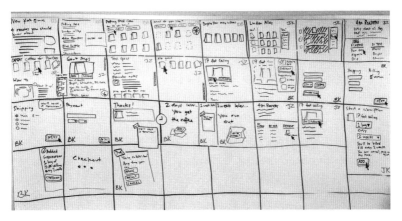

Blue Bottle Coffee's storyboard shows all of the clicks required to select and order coffee beans.

Detail from Savioke's storyboard, showing the robot delivery at the guest's door.

Keep the story fifteen minutes or less.

Make sure the whole prototype can be tested in about fifteen minutes. That might seem short, especially since your customer interviews will be sixty minutes long. But you'll have to allow time for your customers to think aloud and answer your questions—not to mention starting up the interview at the beginning and winding it down at the end. Fifteen minutes will take longer than fifteen minutes. And there's another, practical reason for this limit. Sticking to fifteen minutes will ensure that you focus on the most important solutions—and don't bite off more than you can prototype. (A rule of thumb: Each storyboard frame equals about one minute in your test.)

Once you've incorporated all of the winning sketches, the storyboard will be complete. And you've finished with the hardest part of the sprint. The decisions are made, the plan for your prototype is ready, and Wednesday is a wrap.

FACILITATOR NOTES

Don't Drain the Battery

Decisions take willpower, and you only have so much to spend each day. You can think of willpower like a battery that starts the morning charged but loses a sip with every decision (a phenomenon called "decision fatigue"). As Facilitator, you've got to make sure that charge lasts till 5 p.m.

Wednesday is one decision after another, and it's all too easy to drain the battery. By following the Sticky Decision process and steering the team from inventing new ideas, you should be able to make it to 5 p.m. without running out of juice.

But you'll have to be mindful. Watch out for discussions that aren't destined for a quick resolution. When you spot one, push it onto the Decider:

"This is a good discussion, but there's still a lot to cover today. Let's have the Decider make the call so we can move on."

And:

"Let's just trust the Decider on this one."

Smaller details—such as design or wording—can be pushed off until Thursday:

"Let's leave it up to whoever makes this part of the prototype tomorrow."

If anyone, even the Decider him- or herself, starts to invent solutions on the spot, ask that person to wait until after the sprint to explore new ideas:

"It seems like we're coming up with new ideas right now.

These ideas are really interesting, and I think you should make note of them so they don't get lost—but to get the sprint finished, we have to focus on the good ideas we already have."

That last one is especially tough. Nobody loves stamping on inspiration, and those new ideas might appear stronger than the ones in your sketches. Remember that most ideas sound better in the abstract, so they may not be that good. But even if one of those new ideas is the best idea ever, you don't have time to back up in the process.

Your winning sketches deserve a chance to be tested. If those new ideas and improvements are truly worthwhile, they'll be there next week.

Thursday

On Wednesday, you and your team created a storyboard. On Thursday, you'll adopt a "fake it" philosophy to turn that storyboard into a realistic prototype. In the next chapters, we'll explain the mindset, strategy, and tools that make it possible to build that prototype in just seven hours.

13

Fake It

A square-jawed cowboy stands outside a saloon. He adjusts his hat and squints across the dusty street, where five men in black suits sit on horseback, rifles clutched in their hands. Farther down the street, the townspeople huddle near the general store. A tumbleweed blows by. Nobody speaks, but everybody knows: There's about to be some trouble in this town.

If you've ever watched an old Western movie, you're probably familiar with this scene. Good guys in white hats, bad guys in black, plenty of melodrama. The town is often the most realistic part of the film: clapboard buildings, wooden boardwalks, and saloons with swinging doors.

Of course, those Old West scenes were never quite as real as they appeared. Sometimes, the director found an existing location that looked about right: an abandoned ghost town or a picturesque Italian village. But most films were shot on a set on some Hollywood backlot.

That saloon behind the cowboy? Just a façade—an exterior wall with nothing behind it.

It makes no difference to the audience. For the few minutes we see the town, we get lost in the story. It all appears real. Whether it's a façade or a ghost town, the illusion works.

Thursday is about illusion. You've got an idea for a great solution. Instead of taking weeks, months, or, heck, even *years* building that solution, you're going to fake it. In one day, you'll make a prototype that appears real, just like that Old West façade. And on Friday, your customers—like a movie audience—will forget their surroundings and just react.

Façades are easier to build than you might think. Let's say you're working on a project that will take a hundred days. And let's say that 90 percent real is real enough to test. Simple math says it'll take ninety days to get to that 90 percent real level, so you should be ready to test in about three months. But we've found that if you only build a façade, you can get to 90 percent on day one.

"Whoa, pardner," you're thinking. As of Thursday morning, you'll have nothing but whiteboard drawings and paper sketches. Do we expect you to create a realistic prototype in just one day? Isn't that impossible? It would be impossible, except that you've already done the difficult part on Monday, Tuesday, and Wednesday. The storyboard removes all guesswork about what to include. The solution sketches are packed with specific text and details. And you have the perfect team, with all the right skills to create your prototype.

Sure, you could take a longer time to build a more perfect prototype—but doing so would only slow down the learning process. That may not matter if you're on the right path, but let's face it—not every idea is a winner. Whether you're taking a risk on a bold idea, or

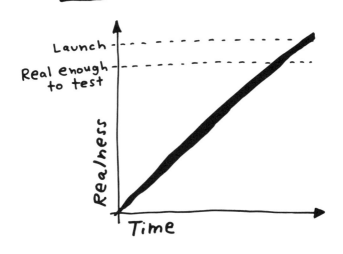

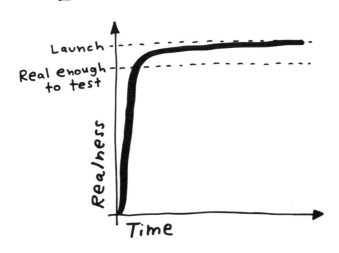

you're just not sure, it's better to find out early. Wasting time on the wrong thing is a major bummer.

But perhaps the biggest problem is that the longer you spend working on something—whether it's a prototype or a real product—the more attached you'll become, and the less likely you'll be to take negative test results to heart. After one day, you're receptive to feedback. After three months, you're committed.

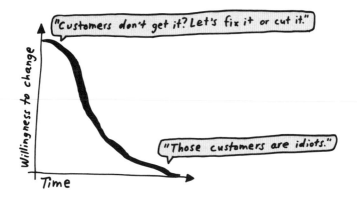

At the beginning, you're in the sweet spot of all these charts (which, to be fair, we made up). You're not attached to your ideas yet, so if they don't test well, you'll be flexible enough to fix or cut them. You're in the perfect position to take advantage of that fast curve to 90 percent real, *if* you limit yourselves to building a façade. No plumbing, no wiring, no structural engineering. Just a façade.

The prototype mindset

Building a façade may be uncomfortable for you and your team. To prototype your solution, you'll need a temporary change of philosophy: from *perfect* to *just enough*, from *long-term quality* to *temporary simulation*. We call this philosophy the "prototype mindset," and it's made up of four simple principles.

1. You Can Prototype Anything

This statement might sound corny, but here it is. You have to believe. If you go into Thursday with optimism and a conviction that there is *some way* to prototype and test your product, you will find a way. In the next chapter, we'll talk about specific methods for prototyping hardware, software, and services. Those methods may work for you, or you may have to be resourceful and invent your own. But if you stay optimistic and adopt the prototype mindset, there is almost always a way.

2. Prototypes Are Disposable

Don't prototype anything you aren't willing to throw away. Remember: This solution might not work. So don't give in to the temptation of spending a few days or weeks getting your prototype ready. You'll have diminishing returns on that extra work, and all the while, you'll be falling deeper in love with a solution that could turn out to be a loser.

3. Build Just Enough to Learn, but Not More

The prototype is meant to answer questions, so keep it focused. You don't need a fully functional product—you just need a real-looking façade to which customers can react.

4. The Prototype Must Appear Real

To get trustworthy results in your test on Friday, you can't ask your customers to use their imaginations. You've got to show them something realistic. If you do, their reactions will be genuine.

How real is real enough? When you test your prototype on Friday, you'll want your customers to react naturally and honestly. Show them something flimsy—a "paper prototype" made up of drawings, or a simplified wireframe of your design—and the illusion will break.

Once the illusion is broken, customers switch into feedback mode. They'll try to be helpful and think up suggestions. In Friday's test, customer *reactions* are solid gold, but their *feedback* is worth pennies on the dollar.

Goldilocks quality

This distinction between feedback and reaction is crucial. You want to create a prototype that evokes honest reactions from your customers. You want it to be as real as possible, while sticking to your one-day timeline. As our partner Daniel Burka says, the ideal prototype should be "Goldilocks quality." If the quality is too low, people won't believe the prototype is a real product. If the quality is too high, you'll be working all night and you won't finish. You need Goldilocks quality. Not too high, not too low, but just right.

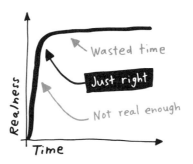

Of course, "Goldilocks quality" looks different for each product. Next, we'll show you some examples: five teams, prototyping everything from iPad apps to a medical clinic. As you read their stories, you'll see how each team applies "Goldilocks quality" and the prototype mindset to their unique challenge. We'll begin with FitStar, a company that had to build an elaborate prototype—and do it without the most important person.

FITSTAR

Question:	How can we explain a new kind of fitness software?
Format:	Simulated App Store and iPad app.
Tools:	Keynote (presentation software), acting, iPhone videos, iPad.

"People are getting the wrong idea. They download the app. They try it. But they think it's something else."

Mike Maser sat back in a plastic chair in our San Francisco office. The brim of his baseball cap was shredded from years of wear, and his plaid lumberjack shirt was faded. Not the look we'd expected for a guy who palled around with professional athletes and spent half his time at video shoots in Los Angeles.

Mike was the CEO of a startup called FitStar. In 2013 and 2014, FitStar's iPad apps would win Apple's coveted Best of the Year awards. In the App Store, FitStar would rank among the top of the charts in the health category, and in 2015, the fitness technology company Fitbit would acquire the startup.

But this afternoon was before all of that, back in 2012, when nobody—except for Mike and his cofounder, Dave Grijalva—quite knew what FitStar was all about. GV had invested in the company, and Mike and Dave spent a week with us. The goal of our sprint: Find a better way to explain their new app.

Mike and Dave had a vision for bringing personal fitness training to the masses. Personal trainers are expensive and tricky to fit into busy schedules. "Most people just can't do it," said Mike. Thanks to Mike's connections in the entertainment industry, FitStar had brought on the best personal trainer they could think of: Tony Gonzalez, a fitness guru and star player in the National Football League. They'd filmed hundreds of hours of Tony giving instruction for different exercises, at all kinds of ability levels. And Dave—a programmer with a background building video games—had created algorithms that stitched together video clips of Tony into custom workout sessions.

They had created an automated personal trainer. It could tailor each workout so it was suited to the customer's fitness level and goals. As he or she progressed, the workouts would adapt and get more difficult. The app had just launched, but FitStar was waiting to promote it until they knew customers could understand how it worked.

So far, people were confused. The message about customization and personalized training wasn't getting through. Most of their early customers thought it was just a workout video, like the old VHS tapes and DVDs hawked on television. "Once you have that mental model, it's tough to break," said Dave.

By Wednesday afternoon of their sprint, Mike and Dave had a slate of promising ideas for improving the initial experience of the iPad app, everything from better descriptions in the App Store to new animations between exercises.

Unfortunately, Mike's favorite idea appeared impossible to prototype. He wanted to record videos of Tony Gonzalez asking the customer questions as he or she set up the app. In real life, when you start working with a personal trainer, the trainer is right there, talking with you. Mike was betting that a back-and-forth conversation would give FitStar the opportunity to explain—in Tony's own words— how customized the software could be.

But Tony wasn't in the sprint with us. He was on the other side of the country, playing football for the Atlanta Falcons. Plus, it would be impossible to build a new version of the iPad app in just one day. And even if we could, we would never be able to get it launched to the App Store in time for Friday's test. We only had one day before the customers came in, and a seemingly impossible prototype to build.

But all we had to do was fake it. On Thursday morning, we divvied up the prototyping tasks. Dave grabbed his laptop and started writing the script for Tony's video introduction. Mike volunteered to stand in for Tony as the on-screen talent. He put on some workout clothes, set up an iPhone to record video, and read lines from the script.

What about the software? FitStar couldn't reprogram and re-release their iPad app in time for the test. But we didn't need a real app. We just needed something that *looked* like a real app. We remembered that you can run Keynote (Apple's presentation software, like PowerPoint) on an iPad. A slideshow running full-screen would look just like an app. It could even play videos.

We divided the storyboard into sections—one for each of us to work on. Then, using both the storyboard and the solution sketches as our blueprint, we built the prototype, screen by screen. We found a template kit online with realistic iPad buttons and icons that we could copy over. We added photos and illustrations from the actual FitStar app to make it more realistic. We dropped the videos from Mike and Dave into the slides.

To complete the illusion, we added screenshots from the iPad App Store to the beginning of the slideshow. These screenshots showed Fit-Star's app in the health category, and even showed the installation process. When we'd finished making all the slides, John took on the job of "stitcher": going through the whole deck, making sure everything looked consistent from slide to slide.

By the end of the day, it looked just like real software—even though there was *no* software at all. FitStar's prototype was just like one of those Old West façades: The illusion only worked for a few minutes, from a certain angle. But that was enough to answer Mike and Dave's big question for the sprint: Can we better explain our app to new customers? After Thursday, FitStar was ready for their test.

Some solutions worked. The videos of Mike explaining the software were effective. Right away, customers could explain the app in their own words ("Kind of an automated personal trainer"), and they were willing to pay for it ("Can I sign up right now?"). Other solutions failed. After the introductory conversation, there was a clip of Dave wearing a lab coat. He introduced himself as "Doctor Algo Rhythm" and went on to explain how the software was programmed. But by that point, customers understood ("I get it."), and they were ready to exercise. They found Doctor Algo unnecessary and even obnoxious (no knock to Dave's acting).

For FitStar, success in the market depended on quality. But in their sprint, success depended only on being real enough to answer their key questions. They got the information they needed to identify the right solutions—and shut down the wrong ones—with a prototype that only took seven hours to build.

SLACK

Question:	What's the best way to explain Slack to non-tech customers?
Format:	Two competing websites with interactive software.
Tools:	Keynote, InVision (prototyping software), the real Slack software, and some acting.

Slack had two competing ideas to prototype. First was "The Tenacious Tour," a step-by-step explanation of the software. Just as with Blue Bottle Coffee, this idea could be faked with a series of slides that looked like a website. No sweat.

But the other idea, "Bot Team," was tricky. It involved a team of computer-controlled "bots" who would send messages back and forth to one another, and even respond to messages typed by the user. To be realistic, the bots should respond to a variety of questions and comments from the customer, an experience impossible to fake with slides.

Merci had the solution: We could pretend to be computer-controlled characters ourselves. During the test, we'd send messages to the user, and—like bots—reply in a not-too-intelligent way. Of course, if the idea proved successful, Slack would have to write computer software to control the bots. They could never have teams of people sending messages to every customer who visited their website. They'd need a staff of thousands, or millions! But for our test, for just five customers, it would work.

THURSDAY

FOUNDATION MEDICINE

Question:	What essential information do oncologists need to make treatment decisions?
Format:	Paper medical report with first page only.
Tools:	Keynote, realistic test data, printer.

Earlier, you met Flatiron Health, a company dealing with the complexities of getting cancer patients into clinical trials. Boston-based Foundation Medicine, another GV investment, was working on a different problem in cancer care: using DNA analysis to suggest possible treatments for patients.

In 2012, Foundation Medicine had developed a test called FoundationOne. The company's lab could analyze a single tissue sample and give doctors a report on every known genomic alteration associated with cancer, along with a list of potential treatments.

The test was groundbreaking. FoundationOne's diagnostics provided a wealth of information, often leading to surprising treatment options. But all that information presented a challenge: It could be overwhelming, even to expert oncologists. In those early days, the FoundationOne results were delivered on paper, and the team at Foundation Medicine was determined to make those sheets of paper as easy to understand as possible. So they ran a sprint with us to try out some new ideas.

The team decided to focus on the front page of the paper report. It was, of course, the first thing a doctor would see when she reviewed the test results. But if the doctor was in a hurry—and oncologists usually are—it might be the *only* page she had time to process. Foundation Medicine wanted to deliver as much information as possible on the top sheet.

In our sprint with Foundation Medicine, we had three competing ideas for the test report. To implement these ideas would require months of work in the lab and a serious quality-assurance effort. After all, medical reports have to be 100 percent accurate. But for our prototype, we only needed to learn which approach was most promising. We didn't need to meet the same accuracy standards that applied to the real report. And we didn't need to alter anything about the lab analysis itself. All of that could come later. For now, our question was about those crucial minutes as the oncologist reviews the front page.

As you might guess, we used Keynote to mock up the reports. We split into three teams of two. On each team, one person was responsible for designing a slide formatted to be the same size as an 8.5-by-11-inch sheet of paper. (A paper prototype is appropriate when—and only when—your final product will also be made of paper.) The other person was responsible for making the information—the genomic data, the recommended therapies, and the rest of the oncology details—realistic and accurate.

If we wanted honest reactions from oncologists, the data had to look legitimate. Of course, testing with real patient data would be unethical. But Foundation Medicine had some realistic-but-not-real test results on hand that they used internally. And the sprint team included experts who could make up more realistic details when needed.

By the end of the day, we had three prototype reports. Each was just one or two pages, printed out from Keynote, on top of a stack of pages from an old, pre-sprint report—a new façade, with an old village in the background. When Foundation Medicine showed the report prototypes to oncologists during the test, they looked just like the real thing.

THURSDAY

SAVIOKE

Question:	How will hotel guests react to a robot with personality?
Format:	Physical robot with iPad touch screen.
Tools:	Keynote, sound effects library, iPad, robot, remote control, hotel room, acting.

Savioke was one of the most complex prototyping challenges we've encountered. We were testing the Relay robot's behavior and personality as it made a delivery: the touch-screen interaction on the robot's face, its movements, its soundtrack of beeps and chimes, and even the timing and script of an automated phone call. That's a lot of moving parts, and some of them were *literally* moving parts.

When a team has an extraordinary prototyping challenge, they often have the extraordinary skills and tools to make it happen. Savioke already had the robot, and most of the behaviors and components already worked. We could build our prototype on top of what they already had. It's like filming a Western in a picturesque ghost town instead of a backlot.

However, there were still four important elements for us to prototype on Thursday. First was the robot's happy dance. Writing code for the perfect choreography would take too long, so CTO Tessa Lau and engineer Allison Tse decided to use remote control instead. On Thursday, they practiced the delivery by driving the Relay robot around using a PlayStation video game controller.

The second challenge was the robot's screen, but Adrian Canoso, Savioke's design lead, had the answer. We could temporarily replace the robot's screen with an iPad mini. The robot's eyes and several simple touch-screen interactions could be faked with a series of slides.

Next, the robot needed a new soundtrack. Adrian had experience as a sound designer. He put on a pair of giant headphones and went to work, using a library of free sound effects.

Finally, we needed to fake an automated phone call when the robot arrived at the guest room. Eventually, this call would be triggered by sophisticated software that tracked the robot's location. For our test, Allison could just watch the robot, then duck out of sight and place the call herself. She just needed to use a stilted voice that *sounded* like a recording.

Now, most teams can't prototype a working robot in a single day. But most teams don't need to—because they aren't in the robot business at all. With the fully operational Relay robot, Savioke had a foundation for their prototype. They needed to make some challenging additions to it, but they had all of the engineering and design expertise required to get it done. By the end of the day, the robot could dance, whistle, and smile.

ONE MEDICAL GROUP

Question:	Can a doctor's office for professionals adapt to families with kids?
Format:	A medical clinic that's only open for one night.
Tools:	Doctor's office, medical staff, bananas, crayons.

One Medical was off to a great start on a bold mission: to offer better health care to everyone. They'd established a network of primary care clinics with locations across the United States—in San Francisco; New York; Boston; Chicago; Washington, D.C.; Phoenix; and Los Angeles. Same-day appointments, treatment via mobile app, more time with patients, and beautiful office interiors had earned them thousands of dedicated patients.

Most of those customers were young, tech-savvy professionals—the kind of folks to whom "treatment via mobile app" sounds like a good idea. That customer base was growing fast, but One Medical wanted to open their service up to more kinds of patients. With plenty of customers starting to have children, the company figured the sensible next step was family care—for the babies, children, and teenagers of its existing patients.

One Medical hoped to serve both families and grown-ups in the same locations. They already had many physicians on staff who were trained in family medicine. But before the first of these new clinics opened, they wanted to be sure patients would have a great experience.

How do you prototype an entire doctor's office? Like Savioke and Slack, One Medical built on top of what they had. Chris Waugh, One Medical's vice president of design, hatched a plan: For one evening, One Medical would simulate a real family clinic in one of their existing offices.

At 6 p.m., the Hayes Valley office in San Francisco closed its doors. Chris and his team went to work. They had several ideas for setting up the office so that it would keep its sophisticated aesthetic—popular with the grown-ups—while adding appeal for children.

They brought in crayons and paper. They set out bananas, apples, fruit bars, and coconut water. They also had a treasure chest filled with toys, but, not wanting to make the lobby feel too childish, they tucked it behind the desk. Two family care physicians were on-site, and two more One Medical employees took charge of the lobby. Everyone had a script to follow. It was time for the prototype.

Then the children started to arrive. Chris had recruited five families to come in for visits. Right away, the test ran into a bump—literally. The doorway at the Hayes Valley clinic had a small ledge that was navigable by wheelchairs but tricky for strollers. "Kids were nearly bouncing out of their seats," Chris said.

The next surprise was how much was *in* those strollers. "Families come prepared. They've got toys, they've got extra clothes, they've got snacks. They bring siblings, grandparents, nannies." The lobby, optimized for individual adults, became crowded. The One Medical team realized they'd need a slightly different lobby design for the family clinic.

The One Medical team had also underestimated the importance of the front desk staff. Kids were nervous as they came in. The clinic was a new place, and young children associate the doctor's office with painful vaccination shots. "We lucked out with our prototype staff. Taleen and Rachel [two of One Medical's office managers] switched into this super-welcoming mode, greeting kids, putting them at ease. It wasn't in the script, but it saved the day."

The exam rooms provided their own challenges. One Medical has their doctors sit behind a desk, encouraging a more natural conversation with the patient than the usual exam bed and rolling chair. But with kids in the room, the desk became an obstacle. "Everything the kids could touch, they touched. Every drawer was opened."

Still, the kids were having fun, so the desks didn't seem like a huge problem. Then Chris and his team interviewed the families. It turned

THURSDAY

out it was the parents—more than the kids—who were bothered by the exam room setup. The parents themselves needed reassurance from the doctor, but the exam room chaos made communication difficult. It was a subtle point, but crucial for putting parents at ease. Luckily, it was easy to fix.

When One Medical opened their first family clinic a few months later, they could see both adults and kids in the same location, and they could staff the office with family medicine doctors from the One Medical team. But there was more room in the lobby, no awkward desks in the exam rooms—and no ledge in the doorway.

14

Prototype

Thursday is a bit different from other parts of the sprint. Every prototype is different, so there's no exact step-by-step process we can share. But after making hundreds of our own prototypes, we've come up with four exercises that always set us on the right path:

1. Pick the right tools
2. Divide and conquer
3. Stitch it together
4. Do a trial run

We'll explain why each exercise is important, and show you how we do each one.

First, we need to talk about your tools—the objects and devices your team uses every day, the software and processes and methods they use to create high-quality experiences for your customers. Here's the challenge: You probably can't use them for your prototype.

Sorry. It doesn't matter whether you work with designers, engineers, architects, marketers, or other creative professionals—or whether you run a store, provide client services, or build physical products. There's a good chance that your team's regular tools are *not* the right tools for prototyping.

The trouble with your team's regular tools is that they're too perfect—and too slow. Remember: Your prototype isn't a real product, it just needs to *appear* real. You don't need to worry about supply chains, brand guidelines, or sales training. You don't need to make every pixel perfect.

The good news is that we were in this same situation not long ago. As designers of software such as apps and websites, we were comfortable with tools like Photoshop and programming languages like HTML and JavaScript. And then we discovered Keynote. Originally intended for making presentation slides, Keynote is a perfect prototyping tool. It has easy-to-use layout tools, so you can quickly make things look pretty nice. It's organized around "slides," which are a lot like frames in a storyboard. You can put in text, lines, and shapes; paste in photos and other images; then add clickable hotspots, animation, and other interactivity. You can even drop video and audio into Keynote when necessary.

We know it sounds crazy, but we're 90 percent sure you should use Keynote to make your prototype. How can we suggest that when we don't even know what you're prototyping? Good question. Of course we can't be *completely* sure—but in our 100+ sprints, Keynote has only come up short a handful of times.

(And yes, if you're on Windows, PowerPoint also makes a fine prototyping tool. It's not quite as nice as Keynote, but a quick web search will yield a number of template libraries you can use to make realistic prototypes in PowerPoint.)

Granted, most of the time, we're prototyping software products such as apps or websites. For these prototypes, we use Keynote to create the individual screens. Sometimes, we run those slide shows full screen, and that's good enough. Sometimes, we use specialized prototyping software* (yes, there is such a thing!) to string the screens together and load them in a web browser or on a mobile phone.

But it's not all software. You read on page 176 about Foundation Medicine, a cancer diagnostics company whose product is a paper medical report. We designed their report in Keynote, then printed it out and showed it to oncologists. (Again, *this* kind of paper prototype actually makes sense.)

For physical products, Keynote will be less useful. You may need to use 3D printing or make modifications to your existing product. But then again, many hardware devices have a software interface. Recall the story of Savioke, where part of our prototype involved attaching an iPad to their robot. And what, you may ask, was on that iPad? Keynote. The hits continue.

Plus, for many physical-product sprints, you may not need to prototype the product at all. One of our favorite shortcuts is the Brochure Façade: Instead of prototyping the device, prototype the website, video, brochure, or slide deck that will be used to *sell* the device. After all, many purchase decisions are made (or at least heavily informed) online or in a sales call. This marketing material will give you a great start on understanding how customers will react to the promise of your product—which features are important, whether the price is right, and so on. And guess what: Keynote is the perfect tool for prototyping that kind of marketing.

We'll admit we're not experts on how to prototype *everything*. And Keynote is not always the perfect tool, especially if you're working on industrial products or in-person services such as One Medical's family

THURSDAY

---

*Software changes fast, so check out thesprintbook.com for links to the latest and greatest prototyping tools.

clinic. But we have picked up some shortcuts over the years. Here's a quick guide you can use to pick the right tools.

Pick the right tools

If you're not sure how to build your prototype, start here:

- If it's on a **screen** (website, app, software, etc.)—use **Keynote, PowerPoint**, or a website-building tool like **Squarespace**.
- If it's on **paper** (report, brochure, flyer, etc.)—use **Keynote, PowerPoint**, or word processing software like **Microsoft Word**.
- If it's a **service** (customer support, client service, medical care, etc.)—write a **script** and use your sprint team as **actors**.
- If it's a physical space (store, office lobby, etc.)—modify an **existing space**.
- If it's an **object** (physical product, machinery, etc.)— modify an **existing object, 3D print a prototype**, or **prototype the marketing** using Keynote or PowerPoint and photos or renderings of the object.

Building a prototype in one day sounds daunting, but when you put together a diverse sprint team you'll have all the right expertise in the room. Chances are, a few people in your sprint will do most of the work, but we've found time and again that there's a role for everyone. Once you've selected your tools, it'll be time to assign some jobs.

Divide and conquer

The Facilitator should help the sprint team divvy up these jobs:

- Makers (2 or more)
- Stitcher (1)
- Writer (1)
- Asset Collector (1 or more)
- Interviewer (1)

Makers create the individual components (screens, pages, pieces, and so on) of your prototype. These are typically designers or engineers, but they could include anyone on your sprint team who likes to feel the force of creation flow through his or her fingers.

You'll want at least two Makers on Thursday. We've told you some wild stories about robots and medical reports and videos, but just remember—the people on your team probably already have the skills to make prototypes for your business.

The **Stitcher** is responsible for collecting components from the Makers and combining them in a seamless fashion. This person is usually a designer or engineer, but can be almost anyone, depending on the format of your prototype. The best Stitcher is detail-oriented. He or she will probably give everyone some style guides to follow in the morning, then start stitching after lunch as the Makers complete their components.

Every sprint team needs a **Writer**, and it's one of the most important roles. In Chapter 9 on page 103, we talked about the importance of words in your sketches. And earlier in this chapter we told you that your prototype must appear real. It's impossible to make a realistic prototype with unrealistic text.

A dedicated Writer becomes extra important if you work in a scientific, technical, or other specialized industry. Think back to Foundation Medicine's prototype of a cancer genomics report: It would have been tough for just anyone to write medically realistic text, so we relied on a product manager with domain expertise to act as Writer during the sprint.

You'll want at least one **Asset Collector** on Thursday. It's not a glamorous role (although "asset collector" does *sound* glamorous), but it's one of the keys to rapid prototyping. Your prototype will likely include photos, icons, or sample content that you don't need to make from scratch. Your Asset Collectors will scour the web, image libraries, your own products, and any other conceivable place to find these elements. This speeds up the work of your Makers, who don't have to pause and go collect every bit and piece they need for the prototype.

Finally, there's the **Interviewer,** who will use the finished prototype to conduct Friday's customer interviews. On Thursday, he should write an interview script. (We'll go into detail about the structure of this script in Chapter 16 on page 201.) It's best if the Interviewer doesn't work on the prototype. This way, he won't be emotionally invested in Friday's test, and won't betray any hurt feelings or glee to the customer.

After assigning roles, you should also **divide up the storyboard**. Let's say your storyboard calls for a customer to see an ad, visit your website, and download your app. You can assign one Maker to create the ad, one to mock up the fake website, and a third to handle the app download screens.

Don't forget the opening scene—the realistic moment that happens before the central experience begins. Be sure to assign a Maker and a Writer to your opening scene, just as with every other part of the prototype. For Blue Bottle Coffee, the opening scene was an article in the *New York Times*, and we needed someone to write a plausible article. (We're not up for any Pulitzers, but faking one short article isn't so hard.)

It's important to give your opening scene enough time to be credible and set the stage. Don't spend half your day working on it, but do make it believable.

As individual sections of the prototype near completion, the Stitcher moves in. It's the Stitcher's job to make the prototype consistent from beginning to end—and ensure that every step is as realistic as possible.

In FitStar's sprint, John was the Stitcher. To ensure consistency, he pasted everyone's Keynote slides into the same file, and then tweaked the fonts and colors so that the slides appeared to be one seamless app. To turn up the realism, he added detail to the sign-up screen, adding a slide with a screenshot of the iPad's on-screen keyboard, to make it look as though the user was really typing.

Stitch it together

Your Stitcher will make sure dates, times, names, and other fake content are consistent throughout the prototype. Don't mention Jane Smith in one place and Jane Smoot in the other. Look for typos and fix any obvious errors. Small mistakes can remind customers that they are looking at a fake product.

The Stitcher's job can take many forms, but no matter what you're prototyping, it's a critical role. When you divide work, it's easy to lose track of the whole. The Stitcher will be on the hook to keep everything tight. He may want to check on progress throughout the day, to see if the various parts of the prototype look coherent. And at the end, the Stitcher shouldn't hesitate to ask the rest of the team to help out if more work is needed.

Trial run

We like to do our trial run around 3 p.m., so that we still have enough time to fix mistakes and patch any holes we find in the prototype. Have everyone pause work and gather around, and then ask the Stitcher to walk through the entire prototype, narrating as he goes.

As you go, you should double-check against the storyboard to make

THURSDAY

sure everything made it into the prototype. The trial run is also a great time to revisit your sprint questions. It's one last check to make sure your prototype will help you get answers.

The primary audience for the trial run is the Interviewer, who will be talking with customers on Friday. The Interviewer needs to be familiar with the prototype and the sprint questions so he can get the most out of the interviews. (We'll explain how to run these interviews in the next chapter.) But the whole team will benefit from watching the trial run. If the Decider isn't a full-time participant in the sprint, now is another good time for a cameo appearance. The Decider can make sure everything matches what she was expecting.

In our normal work routines, there are few days where we begin with a big task, follow a precise plan of action, and end the day finished. Thursday is that kind of day, and it's pretty darn satisfying. When you're finished with your prototype, don't be surprised if you start to wonder when you can do it again.

Friday

Sprints begin with a big challenge, an excellent team—and not much else. By Friday of your sprint week, you've created promising solutions, chosen the best, and built a realistic prototype. That alone would make for an impressively productive week. But Friday, you'll take it one step further as you interview customers and learn by watching them react to your prototype. This test makes the entire sprint worthwhile: At the end of the day, you'll know how far you have to go, and you'll know just what to do next.

15

Small Data

One August evening in 1996, a publisher named Nigel Newton left his office in London's Soho district and headed home, carrying a stack of papers. Among them were fifty sample pages from a book he needed to review, but Newton didn't have high hopes for it. The manuscript had already been rejected by eight other publishers.

Newton didn't read the sample pages that evening. Instead, he handed them over to his eight-year-old daughter, Alice.

Alice read them. About an hour later, she returned from her room, her face glowing with excitement. "Dad," she said, "this is so much better than anything else."

She wouldn't stop talking about the book. She wanted to finish reading it, and she pestered her father—for months—until he tracked down the rest. Eventually, spurred by his daughter's insistence, Newton signed the author to a modest contract and printed five hundred copies.

That book, which barely made it to the public, was *Harry Potter and the Philosopher's Stone*.*

You know the rest of the story. Today, there are hundreds of millions of *Harry Potter* books in print worldwide. How did publishers get it so wrong? Eight experts in children's publishing turned *Harry Potter* down—and the ninth, Newton, only printed five hundred copies. But Alice, an eight-year-old, knew right away that it was "so much better than anything else."

Alice didn't analyze *Harry Potter*'s potential. She didn't think about cover art, distribution, movie rights, or a theme park. She just reacted to what she read. Those grown-ups tried to predict what children would think, and they were wrong. Alice got it right because she actually was a kid. And her father was smart enough to listen.

When Nigel Newton showed Alice the *Harry Potter* manuscript, he got a glimpse into the future. He saw a target reader react to the book before he'd committed to printing a single copy. On Friday of your sprint, you and your team will experience that same kind of time warp. You'll watch target customers react to your new ideas—before you've made the expensive commitment to launch them.

Here's how Friday works: One person from your team acts as Interviewer. He'll interview five of your target customers, one at a time. He'll let each of them try to complete a task with the prototype and ask a few questions to understand what they're thinking as they interact with it. Meanwhile, in another room, the rest of the team will watch a video stream of the interview and make note of the customers' reactions.

---

*In the United States, the book was called *Harry Potter and the Sorcerer's Stone*, due to the fact that philosophers are super dorky.

The FitStar team watches customers use their prototype for the first time.

These interviews are an emotional roller coaster. When customers get confused by your prototype, you'll be frustrated. If they don't care about your new ideas, you'll be disappointed. But when they complete a difficult task, understand something you've been trying to explain for months, or if they pick your solution over the competition—you will be elated. After five interviews, the patterns will be easy to spot.

Now, we know that the idea of testing with such a small sample is unsettling to some folks. Is talking to just five customers worthwhile? Will the findings be meaningful?

Earlier in the week, you recruited and carefully selected participants for your test who match the profile of your target customer. Because you'll be talking to the right people, we're convinced you can trust what they say. And we're also convinced that you can learn plenty from just five of them.

Five is the magic number

Jakob Nielsen is a user research expert. Back in the 1990s, he pioneered the field of website usability (the study of how to design websites that make sense to people). Over the course of his career, Nielsen has overseen thousands of customer interviews, and at some point he wondered: How many interviews does it take to spot the most important patterns?

So Nielsen analyzed eighty-three of his own product studies.* He plotted how many problems were discovered after ten interviews, twenty interviews, and so on. The results were both consistent and surprising: 85 percent of the problems were observed after just five people.

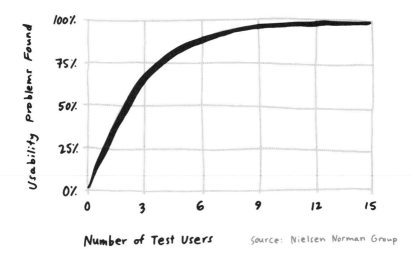

Testing with more people didn't lead to many more insights—just a lot more work. "The number of findings quickly reaches the point of diminishing returns," Nielsen concluded. "There's little additional benefit to running more than five people through the same study; ROI drops like a stone." Instead of investing a great deal more time to find the last 15 percent, Nielsen realized he could just fix the 85 percent and test again.

We've seen the same phenomenon in our own tests. By the time we observe the fifth customer, we're just confirming patterns that showed up in the first four interviews. We tried testing with more customers, but as Nielsen says, it just wasn't worth it.

---

* Nielsen, Jakob, and Thomas K. Landauer, "A Mathematical Model of the Finding of Usability Problems," Proceedings of ACM INTERCHI'93 Conference (Amsterdam, 24–29 April 1993), pp. 206–13.

Remember the door frame in One Medical's prototype family clinic? After seeing two children nearly bounce out of their strollers as they rolled into the office, the problem was obvious. The team didn't need to gather a thousand data points before they fixed it. The same thing with crowding in the lobby and desks in the exam room. When two or three people out of five have the same strong reaction—positive or negative—you should pay attention.

The number five also happens to be very convenient. You can fit five one-hour interviews into a single day, with time for a short break between each one and a team debrief at the end:

9:00 a.m.	**Interview #1**
10:00	Break
10:30	**Interview #2**
11:30	Early lunch
12:30 p.m.	**Interview #3**
1:30	Break
2:00	**Interview #4**
3:00	Break
3:30	**Interview #5**
4:30	Debrief

This condensed schedule allows the whole team to watch the interviews together, and analyze them firsthand. This means no waiting for results, and no second-guessing the interpretation.

One-on-one interviews are a remarkable shortcut. They allow you to test a façade of your product, long before you've built the real thing—and fallen in love with it. They deliver meaningful results in a single day. But they also offer an important insight that's nearly impossible to get with large-scale quantitative data: *why* things work or don't work.

That "why" is critical. If you don't know why a product or service isn't working, it's hard to fix it. If One Medical had put desks in their family exam rooms, parents would have been frustrated. But it would have been difficult to pinpoint the problem. By showing families a prototype clinic and interviewing them about the experience, One Medical found out the *why* behind the problem: Parents needed reassurance from the doctor, and even a tiny bit of distraction was too much. When all you have is statistics, you have to guess what your customers are thinking. When you're doing an interview, you can just . . . ask.

These interviews are easy to do. They don't require special expertise or equipment. You won't need a behavioral psychologist or a laser eye-tracker—just a friendly demeanor, a sense of curiosity, and a willingness to have your assumptions proven wrong. In the next chapter, we'll show you how to do it.

16

Interview

Michael Margolis is an excellent conversationalist. He smiles easily and asks lots of questions, brimming with a natural curiosity about what it's like to live where you live, work where you work, and do whatever it is that you do. It's only afterward that you realize *you* were talking the whole time and learned little about him.

Michael's friendliness and curiosity are genuine, but his conversational skills aren't just a natural gift. Michael is a research partner at GV, and when you watch him interviewing customers—which we've seen him do hundreds of times—you realize it's a practiced art. Everything from the structure of his questions to his body language helps people think aloud and express themselves honestly.

For more than twenty-five years, Michael has conducted research for all kinds of companies—Electronic Arts, Alcoa, Sun Microsystems, Maytag, Unilever, Walmart.com, and Google. Since 2010, he's been at GV, working with the startups in our portfolio.

Over the years, Michael has adapted his research methods to be fast enough for startups, and learnable for the people who work there. Michael has trained product managers, engineers, designers, salespeople, and countless others in how to conduct these interviews. Anyone can do it—even a CEO.

In this chapter, we'll let you in on some of Michael's secrets. Back on Tuesday, you learned his shortcuts for recruiting the perfect target customers (see pages 119–123). In this chapter, you'll learn how to interview. These interviews can teach you about the people who use your product, reveal hidden problems with your solutions, *and* uncover the "why" behind it all.

No matter what kind of customer he's talking to, or what kind of prototype he's testing, Michael uses the same basic structure: the Five-Act Interview.

The Five-Act Interview

This structured conversation helps the customer get comfortable, establishes some background, and ensures that the entire prototype is reviewed. Here's how it goes:

1. **A friendly welcome** to start the interview
2. A series of general, open-ended **context questions** about the customer
3. **Introduction to the prototype(s)**
4. Detailed **tasks** to get the customer reacting to the prototype
5. A **quick debrief** to capture the customer's overarching thoughts and impressions

Friday's action takes place in two rooms. In the sprint room, the team watches the interviews over live video. (Nothing sneaky here. You'll get the customer's permission to record and play the video.) The interview itself takes place in another, smaller room—which we cleverly call the "interview room."

There's no special tech setup required. We use a regular laptop with a webcam and simple video meeting software to share the video and audio. This arrangement works for websites, but it also works for mobile devices, robots, and other hardware—just point the webcams at what you want to see.

Michael Margolis conducting an interview. He sits beside the customer, but gives her plenty of space. A webcam streams video of the customer's reaction to the sprint room.

As complicated as it gets: When testing mobile apps or hardware devices, we use a document camera connected to a laptop. Video streams from the laptop to the sprint room.

Sometimes the Interviewer or the customer are in another building, another city, or out in the field (Michael has conducted interviews at hospitals, hotels, and truck stops), but since the sprint team is watching over video, that doesn't matter. What does matter is that the Interviewer and the customer are sitting side by side, talking comfortably. The interview is a not a group exercise; it's a conversation between two people. One person from your team can be the Interviewer for the entire day, or two people can alternate. (Since you're looking for big, obvious patterns, you don't have to worry about tainting the data with this kind of small change.)

Act 1: Friendly welcome

People need to feel comfortable to be open, honest, and critical. So the first job of the Interviewer is to welcome the customer and put her at ease. That means a warm greeting and friendly small talk about the weather. It also means smiling a lot. (If you're not in the mood to smile, prepare for the interview by listening to "Keep A-Knockin'" by Little Richard.)

Once the customer is comfortably seated in the interview room, the Interviewer should say something like:

> "Thanks for coming in today! We're always trying to improve our product, and getting your honest feedback is a really important part of that.
>
> "This interview will be pretty informal. I'll ask a lot of questions, but I'm not testing you—I'm actually testing this product. If you get stuck or confused, it's not your fault. In fact, it helps us find problems we need to fix.
>
> "I'll start by asking some background questions, then I'll show you some things we're working on. Do you have any questions before we begin?"

The Interviewer should also ask the customer if it's okay to record and watch the video of the interview, and he or she should make sure the customer signs any legal paperwork insisted on by your lawyers. (We use a simple one-page form for nondisclosure, permission to record, and invention assignment. These forms can also be signed electronically before the interview.)

Act 2: Context questions

After the introduction, you'll be eager to bring out the prototype. Not so fast. Instead, start slow by asking some questions about the customer's life, interests, and activities. These questions help build rapport, but they also give you context for understanding and interpreting your customer's reactions and responses.

A great series of context questions starts with small talk and transitions into personal questions relevant to the sprint. If you do it right, customers won't realize the interview has started. It will feel just like natural conversation.

In our sprint with FitStar, we knew it would be helpful to understand more about each customer's approach to exercise. Michael's context questions went something like this:

"What kind of work do you do?"

"For how long have you been doing that?"

"What do you do when you're not working?"

"What do you do to take care of yourself? To stay in shape? To stay active?"

"Have you used any apps or websites or other things to help with fitness? Which ones?"

"What did you want them to do for you? What do you like or dislike about them? Did you pay for them? Why? Why not?"

As you can see, Michael started with generic small talk ("What kind of work do you do?") then steered the topic to fitness ("What do you do to take care of yourself?"). As he asked each open-ended question, he encouraged answers with smiles, nods, and eye contact.

At minimum, these context questions make the customer more comfortable and forthcoming. But quite often, the answers help you understand how your product or service fits into the customer's life—and perhaps, what people think about your competition. In the FitStar interviews, we learned about customers' experience with workout videos and personal trainers, and how they exercised when they traveled—all useful information.

Act 3: Introduce the prototype(s)

Now you're ready to get the customer started on the prototype. Michael begins by saying:

"Would you be willing to look at some prototypes?"

By asking for permission, he reinforces the status relationship: The customer is doing *him* a favor, not the other way around, and it is the prototype that will be tested, not the customer. It's also important to say:

> "Some things may not work quite right yet—if you run into something that's not working, I'll let you know."

Of course, if you built a "Goldilocks quality" prototype on Thursday, the customer will forget it isn't real once they start using it. However, introducing it this way encourages them to give blunt feedback. Explaining that it's a prototype also makes the Interviewer's job easier in case something breaks or the customer encounters a dead end (both of which are likely to happen).

Remind the customer that you're testing the prototype—not her:

> "There are no right or wrong answers. Since I didn't design this, you won't hurt my feelings or flatter me. In fact, frank, candid feedback is the most helpful."

That "I didn't design this" line is important, because it's easier for customers to be honest if they don't think the Interviewer is emotionally invested in the ideas. Hopefully the Interviewer avoided working on the prototype on Thursday—but he should probably say "I didn't design this" even if he actually did. Don't worry, we won't tell on you.

The Interviewer should also remind the customer to think aloud:

> "As we go, please think aloud. Tell me what you're trying to do and how you think you can do it. If you get confused or don't understand something, please tell me. If you see things you like, tell me that, too."

Thinking aloud makes the interview format especially powerful. Seeing where customers struggle and where they succeed with your prototype is useful—but hearing their thoughts as they go is invaluable.

Act 4: Tasks and nudges

In the real world, your product will stand alone—people will find it, evaluate it, and use it without you there to guide them. Asking target customers to do realistic tasks during an interview is the best way to simulate that real-world experience.

Good task instructions are like clues for a treasure hunt—it's no fun (and not useful) if you're told where to go and what to do. You want to watch customers figure out the prototype on their own. As an example, here's the task from the FitStar test:

> "Let's say you came across FitStar in the App Store. How would you decide if you wanted to try it?"

Starting from this simple nudge, the customer reads and evaluates the app description, installs the app, and tries it out. The "how would you decide?" phrasing encourages her to act naturally along the way.

We learned much more from this simple task than we would have if Michael had micromanaged her at every step. ("Install the app. Now sign up. Now fill in your name.") Open-ended tasks lead to interesting interviews. Overly specific tasks are boring for both the customer and the sprint team.

As the customer goes through the task, the Interviewer should ask questions to help her think aloud:

> "What is this? What is it for?"
> "What do you think of that?"
> "What do you expect that will do?"

"So, what goes through your mind as you look at this?"

"What are you looking for?"

"What would you do next? Why?"

These questions should be easy to answer and not intimidating. The Interviewer tries to keep the customer moving and thinking aloud, not anxious to find the right answer.

Act 5: Quick debrief

To wrap up the interview, ask a few debrief questions. You'll see and hear a lot during each interview, and it can be tough to pick out the most important reactions, successes, and failures. When you ask debrief questions, your customers can help you sift through everything you heard.

Here are some of Michael's debrief questions:

"How does this product compare to what you do now?"

"What did you like about this product? What did you dislike?"

"How would you describe this product to a friend?"

"If you had three magic wishes to improve this product, what would they be?"

Don't worry—asking the "magic wishes" question doesn't mean you're turning your product planning over to your customers. Instead, it helps customers articulate their reactions. It will still be up to you to decide how to interpret and apply what you learn.

If you're testing two or more prototypes in your interviews, review each one (to refresh the customer's memory) and ask these questions:

"How would you compare those different products? What are
the pros and cons?"

"Which parts of each would you combine to create a new,
better version?"

"Which one worked better for you? Why?"

And that's it. When the interview is over, the Interviewer thanks
the customer, gives her a gift card, and shows her out.

Throughout the session, the Interviewer should remain engaged in
the conversation. He should encourage the customer to talk while remaining neutral (say things like "uh-huh" and "mmm hmm," not "great!"
and "good job!") There's no need to take notes. The rest of the team in
the sprint room will take care of that for you.

Of course, we don't expect anyone to memorize every question
and all five acts. On Thursday, the Interviewer can start early by writing up a script while the rest of the team is prototyping. On Friday,
he can make a printout to refer to as the interview goes along. Not
only will the script make the interviews easier to run, it will also make
them consistent—which makes it easier to spot patterns throughout
the day.

One of our favorite stories about the power of interviews comes from
our friend, a designer named Joe Gebbia. Back in 2008, Joe and a couple of friends founded a startup. They had what they thought was an
amazing idea for a new online marketplace. They built and launched a
website, then spent months improving it until they were pretty sure it
was perfect.

But despite their efforts, the new service wasn't catching on. They
had a few customers and a little revenue, but they weren't growing,
and—bringing in just $200 a week—they weren't even making enough
to pay the rent. Hoping they could turn the business around before run-

ning out of money, the founders took a somewhat desperate measure. They stopped their engineering work, left the office, and tracked down a handful of their customers. Then they interviewed them. One at a time, face-to-face, they watched people use their website.

Joe describes those interviews as "agonizing and enlightening." He recalls, "We were, like, smacking our heads." Their website was riddled with flaws. Even simple issues—such as picking a date on a calendar—confused people.

When they returned to the office, Joe and his cofounders spent a week fixing the most glaring problems, and then released a new version to their customers. Revenue doubled to $400 a week, and Joe checked to make sure it wasn't a bug in their accounting system. But the numbers were real. So they did another round of interviews, and another round of improvements. Revenue doubled again to $800, then $1,600, then $3,200 a week. That growth didn't stop.

That startup was Airbnb. Today, the online hospitality marketplace operates in more than 30,000 cities and 190 countries. They've served more than 35 million guests. It turns out it *was* an amazing idea, but to make it work, they had to do those interviews. "There's this gap between the vision and the customer," Joe says. "To make the two fit, you have to talk to people."

Airbnb's interviews showed the founders how the product looked through their customers' eyes, revealing problems the founders themselves couldn't see. Listening to customers didn't mean abandoning their vision. Instead, it gave them the knowledge they needed to combine with that vision, so they could close the gap and make a product that worked for real people.

We can't promise that your interviews will make you as successful as Airbnb, but we can promise that the process will be enlightening. In the next chapter, we'll talk about how to make sense of what you observe: taking notes, finding patterns, and drawing conclusions about next steps.

FRIDAY

With a Five-Act script, your interviews are sure to be effective. However, there are a few more techniques Michael uses to make them even better.

1. Be a good host

For just a moment, imagine you are the target customer who comes in for an interview. You've shown up to try some new product (you're not quite sure what) in a building you've never been to before, and you'll be watched by some person you just met. This encounter might have seemed like a good idea a couple of hours ago, but now you're not so sure.

The Interviewer is the host, and the customer is the guest. Michael makes sure the customer is comfortable before the interview begins. He smiles a lot. He's mindful of his body language. He munches on mints so his breath will be fresh. And he always starts with questions designed to put the customer at ease.

2. Ask open-ended questions

To understand what the customer thinks, you have to be careful not to ask leading questions. Some leading questions are obvious and easy to avoid (we're sure you won't say "You like this, right?"). But sometimes, you'll ask a leading question without meaning to do so.

Let's say you're interviewing a customer who's looking at your website—you want to know what the customer thinks, and whether she would be likely to sign up for a demo of your product.

> **Interviewer:** "Now that you've seen the site, would you be ready to sign up now, or do you need more information?"
> **Customer:** "Um, I guess I'd need more info . . . Oh, here's the FAQ. I'll check it out."

This exchange looks okay at a glance, but the multiple-choice question ("ready to sign up" versus "need more information") has influenced the customer's response. You're assuming that the customer wants to do one of those two options. It's tough to do, but you should avoid asking multiple-choice questions. They're almost always leading questions in disguise.

Now, consider what would happen if you ask an open-ended question instead.

> **Interviewer:** "Now that you've seen the site, what are you thinking?"
> **Customer:** "I dunno, I mean . . . I don't think it's right for my company."
> **Interviewer:** "Why is that?"
> **Customer:** (Insert fascinating reason here.)

We just made this scenario up, but it's something we've seen play out dozens of times. When you ask an open-ended question, you're more likely to get an honest reaction and an explanation of why.

All of this may sound a little complicated, but Michael's advice to avoid leading questions comes down to just two rules:

DON'T ask multiple choice or "yes/no" questions.
("Would you . . . ?" "Do you . . ?" "Is it . . . ?")

DO ask "Five Ws and One H" questions.
("Who . . . ?" "What . . . ?" "Where . . . ?"
"When . . . ?" "Why . . . ?" "How . . . ?")

As with everything, asking questions like these gets easier with practice. One simple trick for the Interviewer: Write some sample "Five Ws" questions right into the script.

3. Ask broken questions
Michael Margolis is the master of broken questions. The idea behind a broken question is to start asking a question—but let your speech trail off before you say anything that could bias or influence the answer.

Customer: "Hmm!"
Michael: "So, what . . . is . . ." (Trails off into silence.)
Customer: "Well, I was just surprised to see that the prices were so high."

Michael got an honest, useful response out of the customer without even asking a real question. And because the question was so vague, she didn't feel pressure to tell Michael what she thought he wanted to hear.

In a situation like the example above, where the customer is reacting to something but not saying what, it's tempting to ask a leading question like "Were you looking at the pricing there?" With a broken question, you can encourage people to think aloud, without leading them in any direction.

You can also learn a lot by just remaining quiet. Don't always feel compelled to fill the silence with conversation. Stop and watch and wait and listen.

4. Curiosity mindset

Our final bit of advice on how to be a great Interviewer is not a technique, but a state of mind. On Thursday, the team has to be in a prototype mindset. On Friday, the team, and especially the Interviewer, should work hard at adopting a curiosity mindset.

Being in a curiosity mindset means being fascinated by your customers and their reactions. You can develop this mindset by focusing on the surprising details of what your customers say and do. Always ask "why?" Never assume or jump to conclusions. Before each interview, anticipate how interesting the information will be that you'll learn from the customer. Use your own body language to make yourself friendlier and more receptive: smile, lean in, and don't cross your arms. Curiosity is an outlook that can be embodied, and even learned.

If you'd like to learn more about customer interviews (and see a video of Michael conducting an interview), check out thesprintbook.com.

FRIDAY

17

Learn

It was 8:30 a.m. on Friday morning in San Francisco, the final day of our sprint with Slack. Michael had scheduled our first customer interview for 9 a.m., and the sprint team was trickling in, coffee cups in hand. We rearranged the couches and chairs so everyone could face the video screen at the front of the room. Braden connected a laptop to the screen, opened a web browser, and joined a video conference that Michael had set up.

Slack started the week with a big challenge: their software was hard to explain to potential customers. Many of the benefits of using Slack (better communication, better teamwork, less stress about work) were only apparent once customers took a chance and tried it with their teams. Experimenting with a new piece of software is a lot of work, so Slack had to make the value clear from the beginning.

By Friday of our sprint, we had two competing solutions. Merci

Grace, Slack's product manager, favored a step-by-step guide called "The Tenacious Tour" that would show customers how Slack worked. Stewart Butterfield, Slack's founder and CEO, had a hunch about an idea called "Bot Team"—a way for customers to try out Slack by communicating with a team of computer-controlled characters. You know this story, but you don't know how it ends.

That's what Friday is all about—finding the end to your sprint story. It's your chance to put your prototypes in front of real customers, see how they react, answer your sprint questions, and make a plan for what to do next. On that Friday, everyone was excited and a bit nervous to see how the prototypes would do. A buzz of quiet chatter stopped when the screen flickered to life.

Over the video stream, we heard a door close. Michael's voice began, "Thanks again for coming in today." Then we saw the first customer sit down, nervously look right into the camera, and relax as Michael asked a few warm-up questions.

Michael introduced the customer to our first prototype. For a moment, the customer did nothing, and then she leaned forward, grabbed the computer mouse, and started talking.

Friday feels like one long mystery. Throughout the day, you'll collect clues. Some of those clues help you crack the case, but some lead you in the wrong direction. It's only at the end—around 5 p.m.—that everything ties together and the answers become clear.

Just like the Slack team, your sprint team will spend Friday together. While the Interviewer is testing the prototype with customers, your team will gather in the sprint room to watch and take notes. It's the end of an intense week, and your team might feel pressure to get back to "normal work"—emails, meetings, and mission-critical water cooler conversation. But the sprint only works if you stick together until the end.

FRIDAY

Watch together, learn together

Everybody has a superpower. A unique strength. For software engineers, it's writing code. For marketers, it might be designing campaigns. For us, it's putting sticky notes on whiteboards. There's one skill that you're especially good at, and you probably feel most productive when you're doing that one thing.

It's tempting to disband the sprint group on Friday and let everyone return to his or her superpower. That way, the Interviewer can use his interviewing superpower to test your prototype with customers. We've tried this approach, and here's how it goes: The Interviewer talks to each customer. Good so far. Unfortunately, he can't talk and take detailed notes at the same time, so he records the conversations. The interviews are on Friday, so the soonest he can listen to those recordings is Monday. The interviews take all day, so it takes another full day to review the recordings and make sense of what he heard. Then he needs a few hours to put together a document or presentation with his findings. Now it's Tuesday. (We even know some researchers who edit together a video "highlight reel" of the most interesting moments from the interviews—awesome, but time-consuming.) And once all that's done, the Interviewer needs to schedule time with the sprint team to present and review the findings. At the earliest, it will be the Wednesday after the sprint before the team sees the results.

There are other problems. As time passes, the team's momentum will disintegrate as everyone gets sucked into the vortex of business as usual. And there's a credibility problem, too. Because the team didn't witness the test, they're stuck trusting the Interviewer's process and results. It's like the difference between watching a movie yourself and just having someone tell you about it.

Luckily, the solution to all these problems is simple: Watch the interviews together. It's much faster, because everyone is absorbing the results at once. Your conclusions will be better as a group, since you have seven brains working together. You'll avoid problems of credibility and trust, because each sprinter can see the results with his or her own eyes. And at the end of the day, your team can make an informed decision about what to do next—the results of the interviews (and the sprint) are still clear in everyone's short-term memory.

This wonderful teamwork doesn't happen by itself, but with a few simple steps, you can create it every time. Here's what to do:

Take interview notes as a group

Before the first interview begins, draw a grid on a large whiteboard in the sprint room. Create five columns—one for each customer you'll be interviewing—and a few rows—one for each prototype, or section of the prototype, or sprint question you're trying to answer.

	Tish	Gene	Holly	Luke	Flynn
Marketing page					
Sign up					
First experience					

Distribute sticky notes and whiteboard markers to everyone in the room. Give everyone instructions for how to take notes during the interviews: "When you hear or see something interesting, write it down on a sticky note. You can write down quotes, observations, or your interpretation of what happened."

Use a different color marker depending on the note: green for positive, red for negative, black for neutral. If you only have black markers, write a plus or minus in the corner, or leave it blank for neutral.

During the interviews, the room should be quiet. The interview itself is a time for careful listening and detailed note-taking, not boisterous reactions or problem solving on the spot. It's also important to be respectful of the customer being interviewed. Even though the customer can't hear you (the video should stream "one way") keep in mind that if she struggles with your prototype, it's *your* problem, not the customer's.

At the end of each interview, collect the notes and stick them to the whiteboard. Put them into the correct row and column, but don't worry about any other organizing just yet. Then, take a break. Focusing and taking notes for five hours is tiring, so get some downtime between each interview.

By Friday afternoon, five target customers had tried the two Slack prototypes, and the whiteboard was covered with sticky notes. We gathered around to organize them and look for patterns.

We started by looking at the reactions to "The Tenacious Tour," the solution that featured a straightforward, step-by-step guide to Slack. There was still general confusion about how Slack worked with email, but four out of five customers had understood the overall value—a huge success. Just two of the five had tried to sign up, but there appeared to be many easy-to-fix problems that might improve that number. (One forehead slapper: the "Tour" sign-up button was too far down the page.) Everyone agreed: "The Tenacious Tour" wasn't perfect, but it was way better than Slack's current marketing.

Then we shifted our attention to the results for "Bot Team." Customer by customer, we read the notes. It wasn't pretty. The observations were dominated by comments like "She's confused," "Doesn't seem better than email," and "I'm not really sure what this is." Only one person had enjoyed talking to the computer-controlled characters, and even that person was bewildered by the purpose of the software.

We'd all watched these interviews, of course, but as we looked at the notes, it sunk in: Stewart's hunch had been wrong. That was a surprise—Stewart's intuition was normally excellent—but it was also a relief. Building "Bot Team" and getting it right would have been a big, expensive undertaking. We had given the realistic prototype our best effort, and it had failed. Now the whole team felt confident about focusing elsewhere.

On the other hand, "The Tenacious Tour" looked promising. The pieces were there, and some of the problems would be easy to fix. The next step was obvious. To close the gap, Merci and her team would run another sprint.

The Slack team had hoped for a breakthrough success; instead they got mixed results. But there was good news: they knew "The Tenacious Tour" was an improvement, they knew "Bot Team" was trouble, and they knew they had to focus on the "Slack vs. email" question.

Turning a whiteboard full of sticky notes into a list of patterns and next steps may sound like alchemy, but when everyone has watched the interviews together, it's straightforward.

FRIDAY

Look for patterns

Ask the entire team to gather near the whiteboard. Everyone should stand close enough to read the sticky notes. Take about five minutes to silently review the notes; give each person a notepad and pen to write down patterns he or she sees. Look for patterns that show up with three or more customers. If only two customers reacted in the same way but it was an especially strong reaction, make note of that, too.

After five minutes looking for patterns individually, ask the team to share what they found and read the patterns aloud. On another whiteboard, list every pattern and label each one as positive, negative, or neutral. Once the patterns are listed, it's time to make sense of the results.

Back to the future

On Monday, you came up with a list of sprint questions. These are the unknowns that stand between your team and your long-term goal. Now that you've run your test and identified patterns in the results, it's time to look back at those sprint questions. These questions will help you decide which patterns are most important, and also point you toward next steps.

Slack had two big sprint questions. First, they wondered, "Can we explain Slack to people who have never tried it?" After the sprint, the answer was "Yes . . . maybe." "The Tenacious Tour" had done a decent job of explaining Slack. But Merci and the rest of the team weren't satisfied with a "decent job." They wanted to fix "The Tenacious Tour" and make it even better.

Their second question was "Can we help an individual understand Slack before their team joins?" Every team that adopts Slack starts with a single person. That person has to imagine what it will be like to use the software with a whole team before convincing his or her coworkers to join. The fake team in "Bot Team" was an attempt to solve this problem, and it was a failure. Still, Slack thought there might be a different way to approach this challenge on the marketing page. So they answered, "No . . . maybe," and vowed to try again in their next sprint.

At the end of your own sprint, you'll do the same. Review your long-term goal and sprint questions from Monday. You probably won't answer every question, but like Slack, you'll make progress.

After looking back, it's usually easy to figure out the next step. The team can have a short discussion, and then (you guessed it) the Decider decides how to follow up.

A winner every time

Maybe the best part about a sprint is that you can't lose. If you test your prototype with customers, you'll win the best prize of all—the chance to learn, in just five days, whether you're on the right track with your ideas. The results don't follow a neat template. You can have efficient failures that are good news, flawed successes that need more work, and many other outcomes. Let's look at how five teams interpreted their test results, and what they decided to do next.

Slack had two outcomes from their sprint. First, they had an efficient failure when they discovered that one solution didn't work, saving months of engineering work and extraordinary cost. Their other prototype was a flawed success. Three weeks later, the team reconvened for a follow-up sprint to improve on "The Tenacious Tour." They better explained how messaging worked. They improved their diagrams and clarified the guide. When they tested the improved prototype, the results were stark: The new website was understood by five out of five customers, and Slack built and launched it afterward.

The robot makers Savioke had a sprint with a rare outcome—virtually every idea we tested was successful. Afterward, the team poured their efforts into bringing those ideas to market, and it paid off in the form of great press coverage and new hotel customers.

Blue Bottle Coffee tested three competing prototypes in a classic Rumble. One idea was an efficient failure; the other two were flawed successes. Blue Bottle took the best elements from those two winners and merged them into a website that dramatically increased sales.

Flatiron's sprint question was a big one: Would cancer clinics change their workflow to use a new tool? The stakes were high. If they convinced research coordinators to switch, they could enroll more patients in clinical trials. Working together, we prototyped new software, then tested it with research coordinators. The result was an exciting flawed success. The coordinators didn't love every part of the prototype, but their enthusiastic reaction to the concept gave Flatiron the confidence to continue designing and developing the software. Six months later, clinics were using the real thing to match patients to trials.

Many times, a successful test is not the end of the process, but the beginning. In 2014 we ran a sprint with Medium, a writing platform created by Twitter founder Ev Williams. Ev and his team had several ideas for improving Medium's commenting and discussion tools, and after Friday's test, there were several flawed successes worth pursuing. Medium's engineering team spent the next week building two of the strongest ideas from the sprint. Then, as a test, they launched them to a fraction of Medium's users. It was a follow-up sprint with large-scale data. (It turned out that both ideas increased discussion.)

Many companies want to launch quickly so they can get data from hundreds, thousands, or even millions of people. That large-scale data is great. But in the rush to get there, it's easy to miss the opportunity to gather small-scale data early, when there's still time to course-correct. As Medium's story illustrates, you can have the best of both worlds. You can talk to your customers, *and* you can learn from large-scale data.

Made for people

When you get into a regular rhythm of listening to customers, it can remind you why you're working so hard in the first place. Every interview draws you and your team closer to the people you're trying to help with your product or service.

If you continue running sprints, and if you're true to your vision, the day will come when you'll close that gap. You'll be watching some Friday's test, and you'll see people understand your idea, believe it will improve their lives, and ask the Interviewer how to buy it.

In these moments, it's like Mission Control cheering when the Apollo 13 module safely splashes down in the Pacific. It's like the thieves from *Ocean's Eleven* watching the fountain after the heist, or Gandalf swooping in on a giant eagle to rescue Frodo and Sam. It's amazing. It's what work should be about—not wasting time in endless meetings, then seeking camaraderie in a team-building event at a bowling alley—but working together to build something that matters to real people. This is the best use of your time. This is a sprint.

Liftoff

It's a freezing December day, overcast and blustery. Two cofounders lean close to each other and exchange a few words. One week ago, their latest prototype failed, but they think they know why. They've made a few fixes, and this morning, both men feel confident. After more than three years of building and testing, their crazy long-term goal might be in reach.

A cutting twenty-mile-per-hour wind curls fine spray off the sand. Most people would say the weather sucks, but the two men hardly seem to notice. If their prototype fails, they'll still learn something, and they know that only five people will see it happen. They make the final preparations and check in with the observers. It's time to begin.

And it works. For twelve glorious seconds, everything goes right. Their second test is another success, and the third. Hours after beginning, they run the fourth and final test of the day, and boom! Four-for-four.

In the last test, the prototype works for a full fifty-nine seconds, and the cofounders are elated.

It's 1903, and Orville and Wilbur Wright have just become the first humans to fly a powered aircraft.

It's easy to think of the Wright brothers as otherworldly historic figures whose famous flight was an unparalleled work of genius. But as a reader of this book, you might recognize the methods and hard work that got them off the ground.

The Wright brothers started with an ambitious, practically crazy goal. At first, they didn't know how to get there. So they figured out which big questions they needed to answer. In 1899, the Wrights did their own version of Ask the Experts by corresponding with others who had tried to fly and writing to the Smithsonian Institute for technical papers on aerodynamics. They found existing ideas by researching kites and hang gliders, observing birds, and studying boat propellers. Then they combined, remixed, and improved.

For the next few years, they made progress by staying in a prototype mindset. One step at a time, they isolated challenges and broke through obstacles. Could they get enough lift? Would a person be able to keep an aircraft steady? Could they add an engine? Along the way, they crashed. A lot. But each time, they used a new prototype purpose-built to answer one specific question. They remained fixed on the long-term goal, and they kept going.

Sound familiar? The Wright brothers didn't use sprints to invent the airplane. But they used a similar toolkit. And they used it, and used it, and used it. Forming a question, building a prototype, and running a test became a way of life.

Sprints can create those habits in your company. After your first sprint, you might notice a shift in the way your team works. You'll look for ways to turn discussions into testable hypotheses. You'll look for ways to answer big questions, not someday, but this week. You'll build confidence in one another's expertise and in your collective ability to make progress toward ambitious goals.

The phrase "ambitious goal" might sound like corporate-speak or the headline of a bad inspirational poster. But we shouldn't be embarrassed to have ambitious goals at work. Each of us has only so much time in a day, in a year, and in our lives. When you go to work in the morning, you should know that your time and effort will count. You should have confidence that you're making a difference in real people's lives. With the techniques in this book, you can bring focus to the work that matters.

Since 2012 we've run more than one hundred sprints with startups. That's a big number, but it pales in comparison to the number of people who have taken the sprint process and used it on their own to solve problems, reduce risk, and make better decisions at work.

We've heard about sprints in classrooms. At Columbia University in New York City, professor R. A. Farrokhnia wanted to teach his business and engineering students how to run a sprint, but—with the typical class schedule—there was no way to get a solid week of time. So he hacked the system. Professor Farrokhnia found a free week at the end of summer term and organized an experimental "block week" class that would stretch across the full five days. The typical classroom at Columbia is arranged in auditorium seating, not ideal for a sprint, so he tracked down classrooms being remodeled and hauled in some whiteboards. The sprint was on.

In Seattle, Washington, two high school math teachers named Nate Chipps and Taylor Dunn used a sprint to teach their students about probability. The students created high-fidelity prototypes of a board game in one class period. In the next class, they watched as their peers played the prototype game, making notes about which ideas worked and which didn't. By the time they turned in their final assignment (a revised version of the game), they'd observed how the probability principles operated in real life.

We've heard about sprints in all kinds of contexts. Legendary consulting firm McKinsey & Company began running sprints, as did advertising agency Wieden+Kennedy. The sprint process is used at government agencies and nonprofits, as well as at major tech firms, at companies like Airbnb and Facebook. We've heard sprint stories from Munich, Johannesburg, Warsaw, Budapest, São Paulo, Montreal, Amsterdam, Singapore, and even Wisconsin.

It's become clear that sprints are versatile, and that when teams follow the process, it's transformative. We hope you've got the itch to go run your own first sprint—at work, in a volunteer organization, at school, or even to try a change in your personal life.

You can run a sprint anytime you're not sure what to do, or struggling to get started, or dealing with a high-stakes decision. The best sprints are used to solve important problems, so we encourage you to pick a big fight.

Throughout the book, you learned a handful of unconventional ideas about how to work faster and smarter:

- Instead of jumping right into solutions, take your time to map out the problem and agree on an initial target. Start slow so you can go fast.
- Instead of shouting out ideas, work independently to make detailed sketches of possible solutions. Group brainstorming is broken, but there is a better way.
- Instead of abstract debate and endless meetings, use voting and a Decider to make crisp decisions that reflect your team's priorities. It's the wisdom of the crowd without the groupthink.
- Instead of getting all the details right before testing your solution, create a façade. Adopt the "prototype mindset" so you can learn quickly.

- And instead of guessing and hoping you're on the right track—all the while investing piles of money and months of time into your ideas—test your prototype with target customers and get their honest reactions.

At GV, we invest in startups because we want them to change the world for the better. We want you to change the world, too. To that end, we'll leave you with one more thought about the Wright brothers, this one from their friend John T. Daniels, who was present at their famous flight on December 17, 1903.

"It wasn't luck that made them fly; it was hard work and common sense," said Daniels. He went on: "Good Lord, I'm a-wondering what all of us could do if we had faith in our ideas and put all our heart and mind and energy into them like those Wright boys did!"

We're a-wondering, too. We think you can accomplish a lot, and we know just how you should start.

Checklists

In the following pages, you'll find checklists for every part of your sprint. (You can also find these lists at thesprintbook.com.)

Running a sprint is kind of like baking a cake: If you don't follow the recipe, you might end up with a disgusting mess. You wouldn't skip the sugar and eggs and expect your cake to turn out, and likewise, you can't skip the prototyping and testing and expect your sprint to work.

For your first few sprints, follow all the steps. Once you've got it down, feel free to experiment, just like an experienced baker. And when you find something new that makes the process work better for you, please let us know!

SET THE STAGE

❑ **Choose a big challenge.** Use sprints when the stakes are high, when there's not enough time, or when you're just plain stuck. (p. 26)

❑ **Get a Decider (or two).** Without a Decider, decisions won't stick. If your Decider can't join the entire sprint, have her appoint a delegate who can. (p. 31)

❑ **Recruit a sprint team.** Seven people or fewer. Get diverse skills along with the people who work on the project day-to-day. (p. 34)

❑ **Schedule extra experts.** Not every expert can be in the sprint all week. For Monday afternoon, schedule fifteen- to twenty-minute interviews with extra experts. Plan for two to three hours total. (p. 36)

❑ **Pick a Facilitator.** She will manage time, conversations, and the overall sprint process. Look for someone who's confident leading a meeting and synthesizing discussions on the fly. It might be you! (p. 36)

❑ **Block five full days on the calendar.** Reserve time with your sprint team from 10 a.m. to 5 p.m. Monday through Thursday, and 9 a.m. to 5 p.m. Friday. (p. 40)

❑ **Book a room with two whiteboards.** Reserve a sprint room for the entire week. If it doesn't have two whiteboards in it already, buy some or improvise. Book a second room for Friday's interviews. (p. 42)

Key Ideas

• **No distractions.** No laptops, phones, or iPads allowed. If you need your device, leave the room or wait for a break. (p. 41)

• **Timebox.** A tight schedule builds confidence in the sprint process. Use a Time Timer to create focus and urgency. (p. 47)

• **Plan for a late lunch.** Snack break around 11:30 a.m. and lunch around 1 p.m. This schedule maintains energy and avoids lunch crowds. (p. 40)

SPRINT SUPPLIES

❏ **Lots of whiteboards.** Wall-mounted are best, but rolling white-boards are good, too. Alternatives: IdeaPaint, Post-it easel pads, or butcher paper taped to the walls. Get two big whiteboards (or equivalent surface area). (p. 43)

❏ **Yellow 3-by-5 sticky notes.** Stick with classic yellow, because the multicolored notes cause unnecessary cognitive load. Get fifteen pads.

❏ **Black whiteboard markers.** Using a thick marker will keep your ideas pithy and easy for others to read. We prefer whiteboard markers over Sharpies because they're more versatile, they smell less, and you don't have to worry about accidentally putting a permanent mark on your whiteboard. Get ten markers.

❏ **Green and red whiteboard markers.** For Friday's observation notes. Get ten of each color.

❏ **Black felt-tip pens.** For sketching on Tuesday. Avoid super-thin pens that encourage microscopic writing. We like the medium-point Paper Mate Flair. Get ten pens.

❏ **Printer paper.** For sketching (sadly, not everything fits on a sticky note). Get one hundred sheets, letter-size or A4.

❏ **Masking tape.** For posting solution sketches on the walls. Get one roll.

❏ **Small dot stickers (¼-inch).** For heat map votes. Must be all the same color (we like blue). If you're searching online, these are often called "Round Color Coding Labels." Get about two hundred small dots.

❏ **Large dot stickers (¾-inch)**—For How Might We votes, straw poll, and supervotes. Must be all the same color, and a different color than the small dots (we like pink or orange). Get about one hundred large dots.

❏ **Time Timers.** For keeping time throughout the sprint. Get two: one to keep the current activity on time, and one to remind you when to take a break.

❏ **Healthy snacks.** Good snacks will help keep your team's energy up throughout the day. Eat real food like apples, bananas, yogurt, cheese, and nuts. For a boost, have dark chocolate, coffee, and tea. Get more than enough for everybody.

MONDAY

Note: Schedules are approximate. Don't worry if you run behind. Remember to take breaks every sixty to ninety minutes (or around 11:30 a.m. and 3:30 p.m. each day).

10 a.m.

- ❏ **Write this checklist on a whiteboard.** When you're done, check off this first item. See how easy that was? Keep checking off items throughout the day.
- ❏ **Introductions.** If some people don't know one another, do a round of introductions. Point out the Facilitator and the Decider and describe their roles.
- ❏ **Explain the sprint.** Introduce the five-day sprint process (you can use the slide deck on thesprintbook.com). Run through this checklist and briefly describe each activity.

10:15-ish

- ❏ **Set a long-term goal.** Get optimistic. Ask: Why are we doing this project? Where do we want to be in six months, a year, or even five years from now? Write the long-term goal on a whiteboard. (p. 55)
- ❏ **List sprint questions.** Get pessimistic. Ask: How could we fail? Turn these fears into questions you could answer this week. List them on a whiteboard. (p. 57)

11:30-ish

- ❏ **Make a map.** List customers and key players on the left. Draw the ending, with your completed goal, on the right. Finally, make a flowchart in between showing how customers interact with your product. Keep it simple: five to fifteen steps. (p. 65)

1 p.m.

❏ **Lunch break.** Eat together if you can (it's fun). Remind your team to choose a light lunch to maintain energy in the afternoon. There are snacks if you get hungry later.

2 p.m.

❏ **Ask the Experts.** Interview experts on your sprint team and guests from the outside. Aim for fifteen to thirty minutes each. Ask about the vision, customer research, how things work, and previous efforts. Pretend you're a reporter. Update long-term goal, questions, and map as you go. (p. 71)

❏ **Explain How Might We notes.** Distribute whiteboard markers and sticky notes. Reframe problems as opportunities. Start with the letters "HMW" on the top left corner. Write one idea per sticky note. Make a stack as you go. (p. 73)

4-ish

❏ **Organize How Might We notes.** Stick all the How Might We notes onto a wall in any order. Move similar ideas next to one another. Label themes as they emerge. Don't perfect it. Stop after about ten minutes. (p. 79)

❏ **Vote on How Might We notes.** Each person has two votes, can vote on his or her own notes, or even the same note twice. Move winners onto your map. (p. 80)

4:30-ish

❏ **Pick a target.** Circle your most important customer and one target moment on the map. The team can weigh in, but the Decider makes the call. (p. 87)

Key Ideas

- **Start at the end.** Start by imagining your end result and risks along the way. Then work backward to figure out the steps you'll need to get there. (p. 53)
- **Nobody knows everything.** Not even the Decider. All the knowledge on your sprint team is locked away in each person's brain. To solve your big problem, you'll need to unlock that knowledge and build a shared understanding. (p. 70)
- **Reframe problems as opportunities.** Listen carefully for problems and use "How might we" phrasing to turn them into opportunities. (p. 74)

Facilitator Tips

- **Ask for permission.** Ask the group for permission to facilitate. Explain that you'll try to keep things moving, which will make the sprint more efficient for everyone. (p. 89)
- **ABC: Always be capturing.** Synthesize the team's discussion into notes on the whiteboard. Improvise when needed. Keep asking, "How should I capture that?" (p. 89)
- **Ask obvious questions.** Pretend to be naive. Ask "Why?" a lot. (p. 90)
- **Take care of the humans.** Keep your team energized. Take breaks every sixty to ninety minutes. Remind people to snack and to eat a light lunch. (p. 90)
- **Decide and move on.** Slow decisions sap energy and threaten the sprint timeline. If the group sinks into a long debate, ask the Decider to make a call. (p. 91)

TUESDAY

10 a.m.

❏ **Lightning Demos.** Look at great solutions from a range of companies, including yours. Three minutes per demo. Capture good ideas with a quick drawing on the whiteboard. (p. 96)

12:30-ish

❏ **Divide or swarm.** Decide who will sketch which part of the map. If you're targeting a big chunk of the map in your sprint, divide it up and assign someone to each section. (p. 102)

1 p.m.

❏ **Lunch**

2 p.m.

The Four-Step Sketch. Briefly explain the four steps. Everyone sketches. When you're done, place the sketches in a pile and save them for tomorrow. (p. 109)

❏ 1. **Notes.** Twenty minutes. Silently walk around the room and gather notes. (p. 110)

❏ 2. **Ideas.** Twenty minutes. Privately jot down some rough ideas. Circle the most promising ones. (p. 111)

❏ 3. **Crazy 8s.** Eight minutes. Fold a sheet of paper to create eight frames. Sketch a variation of one of your best ideas in each frame. Spend one minute per sketch. (p. 111)

❏ 4. **Solution sketch.** Thirty to ninety minutes. Create a three-panel storyboard by sketching in three sticky notes on a sheet of paper. Make it self-explanatory. Keep it anonymous. Ugly is okay. Words matter. Give it a catchy title. (p. 114)

Key Ideas

- **Remix and improve.** Every great invention is built on existing ideas. (p. 96)
- **Anyone can sketch.** Most solution sketches are just rectangles and words. (p. 104)
- **Concrete beats abstract.** Use sketches to turn abstract ideas into concrete solutions that can be assessed by others. (p. 106)
- **Work alone together.** Group brainstorms don't work. Instead, give each person time to develop solutions on his or her own. (p. 107)

Recruit Customers for Friday's Test

- ❏ **Put someone in charge of recruiting.** It will take an extra one or two hours of work each day during the sprint. (p. 119)
- ❏ **Recruit on Craigslist.** Post a generic ad that will appeal to a wide audience. Offer compensation (we use a $100 gift card). Link to the screener survey. (p. 119)
- ❏ **Write a screener survey.** Ask questions that will help you identify your target customers, but don't reveal who you're looking for. (p. 120)
- ❏ **Recruit customers through your network.** If you need experts or existing customers, use your network to find customers. (p. 122)
- ❏ **Follow up with email and phone calls.** Throughout the week, make contact with each customer to make sure he or she shows up on Friday.

WEDNESDAY

❑ **Sticky decision.** Follow these five steps to choose the strongest solutions:

    ❑ **Art museum.** Tape the solution sketches to the wall in one long row. (p. 132)

    ❑ **Heat map.** Have each person review the sketches silently and put one to three small dot stickers beside every part he or she likes. (p. 132)

    ❑ **Speed critique.** Three minutes per sketch. As a group, discuss the highlights of each solution. Capture standout ideas and important objections. At the end, ask the sketcher if the group missed anything. (p. 135)

    ❑ **Straw poll.** Each person silently chooses a favorite idea. All at once, each person places one large dot sticker to register his or her (nonbinding) vote. (p. 138)

    ❑ **Supervote.** Give the Decider three large dot stickers and write her initials on the sticker. Explain that you'll prototype and test the solutions the Decider chooses. (p. 140)

❑ **Divide winners from "maybe-laters."** Move the sketches with supervotes together. (p. 141)

❑ **Rumble or all-in-one.** Decide if the winners can fit into one prototype, or if conflicting ideas require two or three competing prototypes in a Rumble. (p. 145)

❑ **Fake brand names.** If you're doing a Rumble, use a Note-and-Vote to choose fake brand names. (p. 145)

❑ **Note-and-Vote.** Use this technique whenever you need to quickly gather ideas from the group and narrow down to a decision. Ask people to write ideas individually, then list them on a whiteboard, vote, and let the Decider pick the winner. (p. 146)

1 p.m.
❏ Lunch

2 p.m.
❏ **Make a storyboard.** Use a storyboard to plan your prototype. (p. 149)
   ❏ **Draw a grid.** About fifteen squares on a whiteboard. (p. 152)
   ❏ **Choose an opening scene.** Think of how customers normally encounter your product or service. Keep your opening scene simple: web search, magazine article, store shelf, etc. (p. 153)
   ❏ **Fill out the storyboard.** Move existing sketches to the storyboard when you can. Draw when you can't, but don't write together. Include just enough detail to help the team prototype on Thursday. When in doubt, take risks. The finished story should be five to fifteen steps. (p. 154)

Facilitator Tip
• **Don't drain the battery.** Each decision takes energy. When tough decisions appear, defer to the Decider. For small decisions, defer until tomorrow. Don't let new abstract ideas sneak in. Work with what you have. (p. 159)

THURSDAY

10 a.m.

❏ **Pick the right tools.** Don't use your everyday tools. They're optimized for quality. Instead, use tools that are rough, fast, and flexible. (p. 186)

❏ **Divide and conquer.** Assign roles: Maker, Stitcher, Writer, Asset Collector, and Interviewer. You can also break the storyboard into smaller scenes and assign each to different team members. (p. 187)

❏ **Prototype!**

1 p.m.

❏ **Lunch**

2 p.m.

❏ **Prototype!**

❏ **Stitch it together.** With the work split into parts, it's easy to lose track of the whole. The Stitcher checks for quality and ensures all the pieces make sense together. (p. 189)

3–ish

❏ **Do a trial run.** Run through your prototype. Look for mistakes. Make sure the Interviewer and the Decider see it. (p. 189)

❏ **Finish up the prototype.**

Throughout the Day

❏ **Write interview script.** The Interviewer prepares for Friday's test by writing a script. (p. 188)

❏ **Remind customers to show up for Friday's test.** Email is good, phone call is better.

❏ **Buy gift cards for customers.** We usually use $100 gift cards.

Key Ideas

- **Prototype mindset.** You can prototype anything. Prototypes are disposable. Build just enough to learn, but not more. The prototype must appear real. (p. 168)
- **Goldilocks quality.** Create a prototype with just enough quality to evoke honest reactions from customers. (p. 170)

FRIDAY

Makeshift Research Lab

❏ **Two rooms.** In the sprint room, the sprint team will watch a video feed of the interviews. You'll need a second, smaller room for the actual interviews. Make sure the interview room is clean and comfortable for your guests. (p. 202)

❏ **Set up hardware.** Position a webcam so you can see customers' reactions. If your customer will be using a smartphone, iPad, or other hardware device, set up a document camera and microphone.

❏ **Set up video stream.** Use any video-conferencing software to stream video to the sprint room. Make sure the sound quality is good. Make sure the video and audio are one-way only.

Key Ideas

• **Five is the magic number.** After five customer interviews, big patterns will emerge. Do all five interviews in one day. (p. 197)

• **Watch together, learn together.** Don't disband the sprint team. Watching together is more efficient, and you'll draw better conclusions. (p. 218)

• **A winner every time.** Your prototype might be an efficient failure or a flawed success. In every case, you'll learn what you need for the next step. (p. 223)

Five-Act Interview

❏ **Friendly welcome.** Welcome the customer and put him or her at ease. Explain that you're looking for candid feedback. (p. 204)

❏ **Context questions.** Start with easy small talk, then transition to questions about the topic you're trying to learn about. (p. 205)

❏ **Introduce the prototype.** Remind the customer that some things might not work, and that you're not testing him or her. Ask the customer to think aloud. (p. 206)

❏ **Tasks and nudges.** Watch the customer figure out the prototype on his or her own. Start with a simple nudge. Ask follow-up questions to help the customer think aloud. (p. 208)

❏ **Debrief.** Ask questions that prompt the customer to summarize. Then thank the customer, give him or her a gift card, and show the customer out. (p. 209)

Interviewer Tips

• **Be a good host.** Throughout the interview, keep the customer's comfort in mind. Use body language to make yourself friendlier. Smile! (p. 212)

• **Ask open-ended questions.** Ask "Who/What/Where/When/ Why/How. . . ?" questions. Don't ask leading "yes/no" or multiple-choice questions. (p. 212)

• **Ask broken questions.** Allow your speech to trail off before you finish a question. Silence encourages the customer to talk without creating any bias. (p. 214)

• **Curiosity mindset.** Be authentically fascinated by your customer's reactions and thoughts. (p. 215)

Observing Interviews

Before the First Interview

❏ **Draw a grid on a whiteboard.** Create a column for each customer. Then add a row for each prototype or section of prototype. (p. 219)

During Each Interview

❏ **Take notes as you watch.** Hand out sticky notes and markers. Write down direct quotes, observations, and interpretations. Indicate positive or negative. (p. 219)

After Each Interview

❏ **Stick up notes.** Stick your interview notes in the correct row and column on the whiteboard grid. Briefly discuss the interview, but wait to draw conclusions. (p. 220)

❏ **Take a quick break.**

At the End of the Day

❏ **Look for patterns.** At the end of the day, read the board in silence and write down patterns. Make a list of all the patterns people noticed. Label each as positive, negative, or neutral. (p. 222)

❏ **Wrap up.** Review your long-term goal and your sprint questions. Compare with the patterns you saw in the interviews. Decide how to follow-up after the sprint. Write it down. (p. 222)

Frequently Asked Questions

Q: Can I facilitate a sprint without any experience?

A: Yes.

With this book, you have everything you need. In fact, you're much better prepared than we were when we started out!

Q: Do sprints require long hours?

A: No.

The sprint requires roughly thirty-five hours of work from each participant. We want the team to be rested so they stay sharp and do their best work. You'll be home for dinner.

Q: Will sprint participants miss a lot of other work?

A: Sort of.

It's impossible to spend thirty-five hours in a sprint and do your normal job. But since the sprint only runs from 10 a.m. to 5 p.m. each day, participants have the option of spending time in the morning to keep up with other work.

Q: Do sprints work at big companies?

A: Yes.

At big companies, it can be difficult to get time from the Decider and other experts. Focus on scheduling cameo appearances for Monday, and be sure to have the Decider delegate another decision maker who can participate every day.

Q: Do sprints work for hardware products?

A: Yes.

The biggest challenge for a hardware sprint will be prototyping. Here are three techniques for creating a hardware prototype in one day: Modify or build on top of an existing product, even if it's incomplete. Use 3D printing or other rapid fabrication techniques to prototype your product from scratch. Or create a Brochure Façade, which allows customers to react to your product without seeing the actual product. For more, see page 185.

Q: Do sprints work for [insert super-hard-to-prototype product or service here]?

A: Almost certainly.

Adopt the prototype mindset and pretty much anything is possible. For more on the prototype mindset, see page 168.

Q: Can sprints work at nonprofits?

A: Yes.

Just like startups, nonprofits have big challenges and limited resources. The definition of "target customer" might be different, but questions about nonprofit concerns like fund-raising, public relations, and community services can all be answered by prototyping and testing with real people.

Q: **Can sprints work in classrooms?**

A: **Yes.**

The biggest challenge to running a sprint in a classroom is scheduling. If you can find a solid week, go for it! But if your class meets only once or twice a week for a few hours each session, you'll have to be creative.

At Columbia and Stanford, professors have adapted the sprint process by having students do one "day" each class session (either in class, or as homework with their team). Dividing the process will create a lack of continuity, and a lot of "boot up" time each session. Help students out by encouraging them to take lots of photos. If possible, let them keep their maps, sprint questions, and other notes on Post-it easel pads or something similar.

Q: **Can we run a sprint with team members in different places?**

A: **Maybe.**

Running a sprint with people who aren't physically in the room is tricky. If you want to include them for Monday's Ask the Experts exercise, or as observers of Friday's tests, that's relatively easy to accomplish with a video conference. But if you want to include them for other steps, you'll need ingenuity and a strong relationship. The bottom line: Nothing that happens on paper or on a whiteboard will work very well for your remote teammates. (Hopefully the technology to solve this problem is just around the corner, but it's not quite here yet.)

Q: **Can I run a sprint by myself?**

A: **Sort of.**

Don't expect a solo sprint to be as good as a sprint with your team. But we've talked to people who have done it successfully, and the techniques for a sprint can be useful on your own. For example, set a timer and force yourself to come up with multiple solutions to a problem. Prototype your ideas to answer specific questions before diving into implementation. See below for more tips on how to use parts of the sprint.

Q: **Can we stop after the "Decide" step?**
A: **No.**

This question comes up a lot, and we know it's tempting. Once you identify promising ideas, you could easily jump ahead and start building them for real. The problem is this: Ideas that seem perfect on Wednesday often prove to be flawed after Friday's test. By continuing with the sprint, and prototyping and testing, you and your team will learn whether those ideas are really as good as they appear.

Q: **Can we run a one-, two-, or three-day sprint?**
A: **We don't recommend it.**

If you compress the schedule, you either won't finish prototyping and testing (see above), or you'll work crazy hours and burn out. Neither is a recipe for good results.

Q: **How about a four-day sprint?**
A: **Maybe.**

If the team has experience running five-day sprints, you may be able to compress Monday, Tuesday, and Wednesday's activities into just two days. However, you should not compress prototyping and testing—allow one full day for each.

Q: **If we've just finished a sprint, can our follow-up sprint be shorter?**
A: **Yes.**

Follow-up sprints are exceptions to the five-day rule. Since you'll already have a map and a prototype, as well as results from your first test to help you create new solutions and make decisions, you can often accelerate a follow-up sprint. Two things don't change: You'll still need a realistic prototype, and you'll still need to test with five customers.

Q: **Can we use parts of the sprint process without running a whole sprint?**

A: **Yes.**

For a big challenge, use a full sprint. But there are lots of sprint techniques that are useful in other settings. If you need to make a small decision in a meeting, try a Note-and-Vote (p. 146). If you find yourselves frustrated by problems, try writing How Might We notes (p. 73). If you're talking about solutions in the abstract, do a Four-Step Sketch to make them concrete (p. 109). Every meeting benefits from a Time Timer (p. 47) and a Facilitator writing notes on the whiteboard (p. 36).

And you can conduct customer interviews (p. 204) at absolutely any time—with a prototype, with your real product, with competitors' products, or even with no product at all. We guarantee you'll learn something.

Q: **Is Friday's test a focus group?**

A: **No.**

A "focus group" is ten or so customers discussing an idea all together, all at once. Focus groups are plagued by the worst of group dynamics: shy people not talking, loudmouths talking too much, sales pitches, and a group-formed opinion that doesn't reflect anyone's honest feelings.

By comparison, Friday's test features one-on-one interviews and observation of customer reactions. In these interviews, you can believe what you see.

Q: Can we run Friday's test remotely, over the phone or by video conference?

A: Yes, but extra care is required.

Our partner Michael Margolis runs remote tests all the time, where he uses video-conference software to share computer screens and interview customers. But this kind of interview is more difficult. You'll need to work extra hard to engage your customer, put her at ease, and encourage her to think aloud. And the technology presents another challenge. You don't want to waste valuable time getting your video-conference software up and running, so practice ahead of time and send your customers a detailed how-to guide for connecting.

Q: Can we test our prototype with fewer than five people?

A: No.

After four customer interviews, it's usually difficult to see patterns. After five, it's easy. (Check out Jakob Nielsen's research chart on p. 198 for an illustration of this phenomenon.) If you schedule five people and only four show up, you might be okay. But don't schedule four or fewer.

Q: Can we test with friends and family?

A: No.

You can only trust the results when you interview customers who match your target profile. Even if your friends and family happen to fit the profile, there's another big problem: They're biased, or at the very least they know too much. In your test, you're looking for honest reactions from real-world customers—something you can never get from someone who knows you.

Q: What about random people at Starbucks?

A: Probably not.

If you're building a product for random people who hang out at Starbucks, this might work. But even so, you'll probably need an additional round of screening to find the exact right five customers—the Starbucks regular, the single parent, the business traveler, whatever.

Q: Should we ever interview customers before a sprint?

A: Yes!

We know how difficult it is to make time for customer interviews before a sprint. We usually can't do it. But if you can, this kind of "pre-research" provides a big head start. It's especially helpful when you're starting from scratch and don't already know a lot about your customers or how they use your product. For example, Blue Bottle was new to selling coffee online, so we interviewed coffee lovers before the sprint to better understand how they shop for coffee.

Q: Are there more resources?

A: Yes.

Check out thesprintbook.com for more information on sprints.

Q: What if my question isn't answered here?

A: We love answering questions about sprints.

The best way to reach us is on Twitter. Jake is @jakek, John is @jazer, Braden is @kowitz, and our team is @GVDesignTeam.

Thank-You Notes

Jake Knapp

First and foremost, thank you to my lovely wife, Holly, for your trusted advice. As my first reader, she helped shape this book—and saved the rest of you from several boring stories. Thanks also to Luke, who taught me the meaning of time, and Flynn, who kept me on task by asking every few hours if the book was done yet.

Thank you to my family: to Mom, for doing projects with me; to Dad, for being in the stands at every basketball game; to Becky and Roger, for tireless support; and to Steve, Rich, Nancy, Karol, Britton, and Mignonne, for putting up with your little brother. Probably the only person in my family who didn't help me even the slightest bit is my nephew, Jack Russillo.

On tiny Orcas Island, I had more excellent teachers than I can list—but a big thank-you to Lyn Perry, Colleen O'Brien, Joyce Pearson, Eric Simmons, Steff Steinhorst, and (of course) Tish Knapp. Thank you to my many mentors at work, especially to Jeff Hall at Oakley; to Sheila Carter, Christen Coomer, Robb Anderson, Melinda Nascimbeni, and Dan Rosenfeld at Microsoft; and to Charles Warren, Jeff Veen, and

Elaine Montgomery at Google. A very special thank-you to Irene Au, for supporting my sprint experiments from the very beginning, and to Michael Margolis, for years of patience and good humor, and for pointing out the positive side of my procrastination.

Thank you to Caroline O'Connor for guidance on the first blog posts about the sprint process and to Belinda Lanks for spreading those posts to a broader audience through *Fast Company*. Thank you to the many readers who ran your own sprints, shared your experiences, and asked for more stories and greater detail. Your interest was the spark for this book.

Many thanks to those who gave early advice on the book project: Joe Kraus, Jodi Olson, M.G. Siegler, Gaurav Singal, Kevin Rose, Scott Berkun, and Josh Porter. Thank you to Tim Brown for your insight and encouragement, and to Charles Duhigg for being so generous with your time.

A very, very big thank-you to our agents, Christy Fletcher and Sylvie Greenberg. Christy and Sylvie are the Obi-Wan Kenobis of *Sprint*. If this book is readable or useful, it is thanks to their expert guidance and ability to put themselves into the reader's shoes.

Ben Loehnen, our editor at Simon & Schuster, can read entire manuscripts in three subway stops and spot a cliché through a wall of solid steel. But his real superpower was making us sound more intelligent than we actually are. Ben, if you ever decide to quit publishing and edit dialogue for everyday life, I'm interested.

Jon Karp at Simon & Schuster provided early and steadfast enthusiasm. Publishing a book is complicated work, and *Sprint* made it into the world with the help of Richard Rohrer, Cary Goldstein, Leah Johanson, Jackie Seow, Stephen Bedford, Ruth Lee-Mui, Brit Hvide, and many others at S&S. And a hand-lettered, UV-varnished, triple-embossed (is that a thing?) thank-you to Jessica Hische, who brought the cover to life.

Like a friend who points out spinach in your teeth, our test readers provided forthright criticism to help *Sprint* look its best. Thank you to Julie Clow, Paul Arcoleo, Mark Benzel, Jake Latcham, Aaron Bright, Kevin Sepehri, Andrea Wong, Jose Pastor, Justin Cook, Jenny Gove, Kai Haley, Nir Eyal, Steph Habif, Jason Ralls, Michael Leggett, Melissa Powel, Xander Pollock, Per Danielsson, Daniel Andefors, and Anna Andefors.

Some thank-yous don't fit into obvious categories. Alex Ingram reviewed the Monday chapters over and over and over again (it was really a mess at first) and helped explain the sprint from a startup's perspective. Sunkwan Kim and Elliot Jay Stocks advised us on print design. Becky Warren suggested the Marie Tharp story. Chip and Dan Heath wrote *Made to Stick*, the book that served as our primary inspiration for *Sprint*. (Keep on stickin', Heath Brothers!)

The entire team at GV was exceptionally understanding and supportive throughout the book-writing process. Thanks especially to Mandy Kakavas, Ken Norton, Phoebe Peronto, Rick Klau, Kaili Emmrich, and Tom Hulme for your timely feedback and suggestions. A very special thank-you to Laura Melahn, who provided brutal honesty and energetic encouragement. And another very special thank-you to Jenn Kercher, who navigated approximately 1,001 legal questions— and caught some well-hidden typos. A diamond-studded thank-you to David Krane for your ideas, advice, and enthusiasm. And an extra special, super deluxe thank-you to Bill Maris, whose encouragement and support made *Sprint* possible.

It is very unlikely that this book would have been finished before the year 2027 without the help of Kristen Brillantes. She organized our time, put up with our chaos, and even listened to a robot voice read the manuscript aloud on a seven-hour road trip. Kristen, you are quite a friend.

From the very first outline to the last detail of the cover, Michael Margolis and Daniel Burka collaborated with John, Braden, and me on this book. They read and reread, provided detailed suggestions and constructive arguments, and convinced me to remove the most un-funny jokes. Michael, Daniel, Braden, and John—it is an honor to work with you.

John Zeratsky

Thank you to my wife and best friend, Michelle. Your love and encouragement make me a better person. I'm so lucky to be stuck with you.

Thanks to my parents, who supported and entertained a huge range of hobbies when I was a child. (This included sailing-yacht design and music production, among other things.) You helped me develop a love of learning that I'm very grateful for.

My grandpa in rural Wisconsin became an unlikely computer geek in the 1970s, and his passion for digital technology fueled my interest. He was more than a loving grandfather. He was a friend, a mentor, and a patient source of technical support.

Thanks to all my friends and colleagues at the *Badger Herald*. You gave me a thorough introduction to design and journalism. Thanks to you, I got to design a newspaper, manage print production, write a column about jazz, and even lead our board of directors.

Thank you to Suzy Pingree and Nick Olejniczak. At the University of Wisconsin–Madison, Suzy and Nick made me feel at home—no small feat on a forty-thousand-student campus. Nick introduced me to blogging and taught me web development. Suzy allowed me to enroll in several of her graduate seminars. They introduced me to my first freelance design clients and provided support beyond words.

In 2005 the FeedBurner team gave me an unbelievable opportunity to jump in over my head. Thanks to Matt Shobe, Dick Costolo, Eric Lunt, and Steve Olechowski for my shot at the big time. I still can't believe you let me do all that stuff.

In 2011 another group of partners gave me an opportunity that I'm not sure I deserved. Thank you, Braden, for recruiting me to join you at GV. Thanks to Bill Maris, David Krane, Joe Kraus, and the rest of GV for embracing design in venture capital before anyone else. I'm honored and humbled to be part of this team.

I have been privileged to work with dozens of GV portfolio companies. Their curious, talented teams gave me the most transformative learning experiences of my career. Thanks in particular to Pocket, Foundation Medicine, Blue Bottle Coffee, Savioke, and Cluster.

To Kristen, Daniel, Jake, Michael, and Braden (yes, you again, Braden): Thank you. I can't tell you what a pleasure it is to work together. Thanks in particular for encouraging me to embrace writing again—almost ten years after I forgot I was a writer.

Finally, thanks to our agents, Christy Fletcher and Sylvie Greenberg, and our editor, Ben Loehnen. You led us from "what if" to "holy crap, this is happening" with strength and poise. And you gave us access to a literary world that we had only seen in movies and TV shows.

Braden Kowitz

Thank you to my parents, who showed me joy in creativity, taught me how to repair almost anything, and let me wander through the wilderness. They gave me a TI-99/4A computer and an accompanying cassette recorder to store my first program, all before anyone thought that was a good idea. I am so grateful to have inherited the joy of exploration from them.

Thank you to all the instructors and classmates at Carnegie Mellon University who helped me understand design and how to use it to make the world a better place. They gave me room to practice and the confidence to make mistakes.

I have been incredibly lucky to be a part of Google for most of my career. In that time I've worked with countless talented and inspiring people who taught me how to make products that people love. In particular, thanks to Chad Thornton, Michael Leggett, and Darren Delaye for keeping me on my toes and always offering sharp, honest, and helpful critique.

To Joe Kraus, thank you for showing me how to help teams come together to build amazing things. Your mentorship and support through the years has meant so much to me.

It's easy to get lost in minutiae and lose track of what's really important in life. Thank you to Om Malik for encouraging me to follow my heart.

My closest friends have listened to me ramble about this book over many miles of hikes and pints of beer, and at every backyard picnic for the past year. Pat, Amanda, Chad, Heather, Kenneth, Brett, and Donal, you are amazing and I love you all dearly.

Most of all, I am grateful for the entire team at GV. Jake, John, Michael, Daniel, and Kristen, I can't imagine a better team for the challenges we've faced or better companions for the adventures ahead.

Image Credits

Christophe Wu took the photos on pages 74, 111, and 113.

Graham Hancock took the Time Timer photo on page 47.

Adrian Canoso designed the Relay robot on page 14.

Heidi Qiao volunteered to sit for the customer test photos on pages 203 to 204.

All other photos are by either Jake Knapp, Braden Kowitz, or John Zeratsky.

Image postproduction by Braden Kowitz.

Illustrations by Jake Knapp.

Index